Claim Your Cash!

How to Collect your Entitlements

About the author

For Steve Wiseman writing is a spare-time activity - in his day job he runs the Norwich and District Citizens Advice Bureau, a thriving advice centre each year consulted by around 57,000 people. This entails day-to-day management, but also fundraising and development to ensure the Bureau meets the needs of the public.

In 2001, Steve completed an MA in Education and Professional Development at the University of East Anglia, the dissertation for which centred around the issue of how people access information and advice on their legal rights and entitlements. This research concludes that people most often use the media, friends and family to get information (perhaps explaining why they get things wrong!), but they would welcome other more accessible sources. The findings are being used to help Citizens Advice Bureaux around the UK, including Norwich, to develop their services.

Steve's other work has included occasional freelance journalism, advice work, teaching, lecturing and a few years as a Whitehall civil servant. He lives in Norwich and is married with two children.

Claim Your Cash! by Steve Wiseman

Published by:
Law Pack Publishing Limited
76-89 Alscot Road
London SE1 3AW
www.lawpack.co.uk

ISBN: 1 904053 04 1

All figures are stated as at 1st November 2002 and may be liable to change in the Budget.

For convenience (and for no other reason) 'him', 'he' and 'his' has been used throughout and should be read to include 'her', 'she' and 'her'.

Contents

Claim your cash

Like thousands of us, you may be eligible for financial help and not know it. Three quarters of all taxpayers pay more than they need to and millions of pounds go unclaimed in welfare benefits and special allowances each year. This book tells you what you could be missing out on.

This handbook contains information on the main payments to which you may be entitled. Each chapter describes how you go about claiming a particular payment and gives some useful tips to ensure the best chance of success. Each chapter also contains an at-a-glance Qualification Checklist so you can work out whether it's worth claiming, and an Amount Box so you know how much you are likely to receive.

In the following summary of contents, you will probably find that more than one category will apply to you. For example, whether you are employed or unemployed, or in poor health or disabled, you may have housing costs as well as children to care for. Also many other cash payments are listed in *In Brief* at the end of the book and any of these could be relevant to you.

Summary of contents

If you are pregnant	Help with living expenses	Statutory Maternity Pay Maternity Allowance Income Support if you are pregnant or have children Milk - free of charge
	Help with other costs	Milk - free of charge Vitamin drops or tablets - free of charge
	If you need help in buying things for the baby	Maternity Grant (Sure Start Maternity Grant)
	To meet the cost of milk and vitamins	Health Benefits

If you are widowed	If, as a result of being widowed, you need help with living expenses	Bereavement Allowance Bereavement Payment Income Support if you are widowed Widowed Parent's Allowance
	If you are widowed as a result of service in the Armed Forces	War Widow's or Widower's Pension
If you are unemployed	Help with living expenses	Job Seeker's Allowance: Income Based Hardship payments Job Seeker's Allowance: Contribution Based
	If you have just found a job	Back to Work Bonus
If you are self-employed	Help with expenses	Self-employment expenses: tax relief
If you are employed	If you increase your hours or start a new job	Back to Work Bonus Child Maintenance Bonus
	Supplementing your income	Job Seeker's Allowance: Contribution Based Job Seeker's Allowance: Income Based Working Families' Tax Credit Working Tax Credit Disabled Person's Tax Credit Income Support (see various chapters)

	If you are made redundant	Redundancy Payments Scheme
	You incur expenses which your employer does not reimburse	Employee expenses: tax relief
Your housing costs	If you need help in paying Council Tax	Council Tax Benefit Council Tax: Second Adult Rebate Council Tax Benefit (Extended payments)
	If you need help in paying your rent	Housing Benefit Housing Benefit (Extended payments) Housing costs - extra help
	If you need help in paying your mortgage and other housing costs	Mortgage and other loans - help with repayments (Income Support) Mortgage Interest Run On
	Help with home repairs or renovations	House Renovation Grant Home Repairs Assistance Central Heating System Grant
	Help with home security costs	Home Security Grant
	Help if you want to let a room in your home	Letting out rooms : tax relief The Rent a Room Scheme: tax relief if you have a lodger at home
Fuel and heating costs	Help with insulation and energy efficiency	Home Insulation and Energy Efficiency Grants

	If the weather is colder than usual	Cold weather payments
	Help with winter fuel costs	Winter fuel payments
If you are caring for children	If you need help in buying things for the baby	Sure Start Maternity Grant
	If you care for a child or children	Child Tax Credit Children's Tax Credit Child Benefit Widowed Parent's Allowance
	If you are bringing up a child because one or both of his parents is dead	Guardian's Allowance
	If you are a widowed parent	Bereavement Allowance
	If you need help with living expenses	Income Support if you are pregnant or have children Milk - free of charge Vitamin drops or tablets - free of charge
	Help with other costs	Milk - free of charge Vitamin drops or tablets - free of charge
	Help with school costs	School Meals Subsidy School Uniform Allowance
	If your child is disabled and needs extra personal care or help with getting about	Disability Living Allowance

	If you are a single parent and you have found a job or increased your hours	Lone Parent Run On
If you are studying or training, full- or part-time	If you need help with living costs	Income Support if you are a student Income Support if you are a young person on a training course
	Help with school costs	School clothing School transport
If you are retired	Help with living expenses	Retirement Benefit: Graduated Retirement Pension - see the various chapters Minimum Income Guarantee Pension Tax Credit
Death	If you need help with funeral costs	Funeral expenses payment
If you have a health problem or disability	If you need help with living expenses	Statutory Sick Pay Incapacity Benefit Disability Income Guarantee Income Support if you are disabled or ill Disabled Person's Tax Credit Working Tax Credit
	If you need help with personal care	Disability Living Allowance Attendance Allowance

	If you need help with getting about	Disability Living Allowance
	If you are disabled and need help with personal care or household assistance	Independent Living (1993) Fund Social Services Direct Payments
	If you need to adapt your home	Disabled Facilities Grant
	If you were injured in an accident at work	Industrial Disablement Benefit
	If you became ill as a result of work	Industrial Disablement Benefit
	If you have a disability caused or made worse by service in HM Armed Forces	War Disablement Pension and other allowances
	If you are disabled because of vaccine damage	Vaccine Damage Payment
	Help with meeting NHS charges	Health Service charges - concessions Health Service charges - help under the Low Income Scheme Health Service charges - claiming exemptions
	If you are registered blind	Blind Person's Allowance
	Parking concessions if you are disabled	Parking concessions
Other situations	If you need help with dental costs	Health Benefits
Going into a care home	Help with costs and living expenses	Minimum Income Guarantee

		Disability Income Guarantee Care homes - help with the fees
Carers	If you care for an ill or disabled person	Invalid Care Allowance (soon to be renamed Carer's Allowance) Income Support if you are a carer
Other situations	If you have expenses difficult to meet out of your regular income	Community Care Grant
	If you have an income and are married	Married Couple's Allowance - to reduce your Income Tax
	If you have an income, whatever your circumstances	Personal Allowance - to reduce your Income Tax bill
	If you pay maintenance	Maintenance payments: tax relief
	Help with meeting contributions to your future pension	Pension contributions: tax relief
	Increasing the pension you will get on retirement	Home Responsibilities Protection
	Increasing your chances of receiving certain benefits later	National Insurance credits
	A bonus at Christmas	Christmas Bonus

Introduction

Getting further help

Working out what you might qualify for isn't easy - many forms of cash help are available, all backed up by pretty complex rules. Even when you know where you stand, the process of claiming may not be straightforward. This book has been written to help clear the confusion and to help you claim the cash due to you.

Where things get complicated, you will see the words Take Advice in the chapters but whether or not these words appear, you may feel you need more information, advice or help with the actual claim. Set out in this book are the places where you can get basic information, and in some cases individual advice on how you stand, including having someone to assist you or act on your behalf if needed.

- You can get information directly from the body dealing with the benefit or entitlement - see the chapters for more detail. If you want to use the internet, www.ukonline.gov.uk is the best link to the websites of most national government departments and local councils, and other government bodies, if you don't know their particular web addresses.

- Your local Jobcentre Plus, Pensions Service, Inland Revenue Enquiry Offices and Citizens Advice Bureau (CAB) or other advice service (maybe also your local council offices and post office) should have some leaflets and forms.

- There are a vast number of national charities that provide free advice and information on particular issues, such as financial help available if you are a student, a disabled person, a single parent or a pensioner. Your local CAB or other advice service will point you in the right direction. It may also be worth contacting the Telephone Helplines Association as they can let you know if there is a telephone helpline relevant to your needs (see *Useful addresses*).

- If you are a member of a trade union, staff or professional association, you may be able to get help from them. Your main public library may also hold a range of books, leaflets and internet access on your entitlements as well as information telling you where to get free advice locally.

- In order to find out about local advice services or solicitors' practices to meet your needs, you could also try the Government's national Community Legal Service directory in your local library or on their website at www.justask.org.uk.

- The Citizens Advice Bureaux will provide advice to meet your needs, and may assist you in pursuing your claim, for example, by helping you to fill in forms or appeal to a tribunal. Bureaux are independent organisations and their service is confidential. They are a popular source of aid so they often have large queues in their reception areas and their telephone lines get jammed. If possible, see if you can make an appointment or get there early! Some bureaux will deal with your enquiries via email. The address of your nearest CAB will be listed in the phone book or you can find out from the National Association of Citizens Advice Bureaux (see *Useful addresses*).

- The work of other advice services will vary from place to place. In order to find out if there is one near you, try your local council or the Federation of Independent Advice Centres (see *Useful addresses*).

- You may also have a Law Centre near you. Staffed by solicitors as well as advice workers, they may offer free specialist advice or act on your behalf. The places mentioned above will tell you if there is one, otherwise find out from the Law Centres Federation for England and Wales, or the Scottish Association of Law Centres or Law Centre Northern Ireland.

- As an alternative you could find a solicitor in private practice. If your income is low (see *In brief*), you may be able to get free or reduced cost advice, but otherwise you will have to pay commercial rates. For the more complex Income Tax matters, especially to do with tax relief, you may be best advised to hire an accountant who specialises in that area. The fees will vary depending on the nature and complexity of the work required.

Ten things you should know about claiming

1. Know where to claim

The chapters tell you where to claim. Mostly this will be the Government or your local council, although in some cases you have to apply to another body such as a your employer or a trust. All the contact information you need is under the *Useful addresses* chapter at the end of this book.

The main government departments involved are the Department for Work and Pensions (DWP) and the Inland Revenue. Several different parts of the DWP deal with different benefits. For some benefits there is one national office to whom you claim, but for others your claim is dealt with at local level. The relevant chapters advise you who to go to. If your claim is dealt with locally, usually the chapter will say that you should claim from your local social security office. In most cases, if you are under pension age, your claim will be to your local Jobcentre Plus office. If you are over pension age, it will be the Pensions Service office. Simple? Not quite. The complication is that these new offices were only launched in April 2002 and at the time of writing the reorganisation is still going on, so you may find in your local area that the Jobcentre Plus is dealing with over pension age benefits as well. The best bet is to take advice or ask at your local Jobcentre, or the office that used to be called the Benefit Agency - you will then be told where to claim. Hopefully the changes will have bedded in over 2003!

2. Know how to appeal

If your claim fails, it's important to find out why you were turned down. In most cases, you will have the right to have the decision reviewed or to go to an independent appeal tribunal, or you may have a complaint about the way your claim was dealt with. If you are not told in writing why you have failed, complain anyway! If you are not sure if you have grounds for appeal or complaint, take advice. Many appeals are successful because the decision makers have misunderstood their own rules or got the facts wrong!

The office you have been dealing with will have a complaints procedure which you can use. With reviews and appeals there is usually a time limit - one month in the case of benefits - and you will have a chance to explain your case to an independent tribunal. A caseworker from one of the advice services, or a solicitor, may represent you - see *Getting further help*. Further advice about complaining and appealing can be found in my book *How to Complain Effectively* (Law Pack Publishing Ltd, 2001).

3. Some payments can affect other payments

As you read through the chapters you will see that there are many forms of cash help available, but they do fall into certain categories. There are those that are means-tested such as Income Support, Income Based Job Seeker's Allowance and Housing Benefit. There are others that depend on your National Insurance record, for example, Contributory Based Job Seeker's Allowance, Incapacity Benefit and Retirement Pension. Then again, a third batch may be paid to you if you are faced with certain circumstances, for example, if you have care or mobility needs - Disability Living Allowance, if you are a carer - Invalid Care Allowance, if you are taking up a new job - Back to Work Bonus. Other claims take the form of tax reliefs on certain activities, such as the Rent a Room Scheme or tax relief on your employee or self-employed expenses.

You may find you could qualify for cash help in different categories. Claim as soon as you can, but bear in mind that receiving some benefits may affect others. This may be good or bad news! For example, if you succeed in claiming Disability Living Allowance, you may also be able to qualify for extra Income Support and your carer, if any, will be able to claim Invalid Care Allowance. If you receive Income Support, you will qualify automatically for free prescriptions. On the other hand, some benefits you might qualify for may cancel each other out. For example, if you qualify for Statutory Sick Pay from your employer, you will not be able to get Incapacity Benefit as well, and your income could be too high for Income Support.

4. Some benefits are taxable

Some of the benefits you receive are taxable which means that you may be asked by the Inland Revenue to pay income tax on the income you receive, just like you would for wages or a salary, for example. Whether you actually pay any tax will depend on the tax allowances and tax reliefs you may qualify for - see the chapters on these. Also see *Tax allowances and Tax reliefs and your Tax Return - some general points.*

The taxable benefits are Statutory Maternity Pay, Statutory Sick Pay, Widowed Parent's Allowance, Bereavement Allowance, Incapacity Benefit, Invalid Care Allowance, the retirement pensions and Job Seeker's Allowance. However, any increases for children on any of these benefits are not taxable.

5. Special rules in special circumstances

You may face extra restrictions on claiming certain benefits, even though you meet all the qualifying conditions, if you have to serve a prison sentence, stay in hospital, go into a care home or if your child is in care. There are also special rules if you or your partner are involved in a trade dispute, or if you are from outside the UK and subject to immigration control (that is, there is a restriction on how long you can stay in the country or on claiming public funds). Take advice if any of these circumstances apply to you. However, there is no bar to claiming if you are a British Citizen, a citizen of an European Economic Area country (that is any European Union country plus Iceland, Liechtenstein and Norway), a refugee, or from the Isle of Man, Channel Islands or Northern Ireland.

Having said this, for certain benefits you may still be barred if you do not normally live in the UK, Isle of Man, Channel Islands or Northern Ireland. Take advice if you feel you are having trouble convincing the benefits offices that you are normally resident in this country; if necessary you may need to appeal.

Some benefits can be still be paid if you go to live abroad, although some will only be paid for a fixed time period.

6. Watch out for overpayment and fraud

When you claim, it is important to declare all the information asked of you. In the case of the means-tested benefits and tax credits, this includes all income and capital. Also, you have to keep the relevant office informed of any changes in your circumstances, for example, if you recover from an illness, or if your income increases, or one of the children you have claimed for leaves home. If you fail to do this and you get found out, at best you will be asked to pay back the benefit you weren't entitled to (maybe over a certain period of time to make it easier for you) but at worst you could be prosecuted for fraud! If either of these things happen to you take advice as you can appeal if you feel you are in the right.

7. You may be able to backdate

On reading this book you may discover cash you could have claimed ages ago! Your claim can sometimes be backdated provided you have qualified for all of this time. For certain benefits this backdating is automatic for three months if you request it, for example, Incapacity Benefit, Industrial Disablement Benefit, Child Benefit, Guardian's Allowance, Retirement Pension, Maternity Allowance, Widowed Parent's Allowance, Bereavement Allowance, Bereavement Payment and Invalid Care Allowance.

For other benefits backdating may be allowed for one month or three months in certain cases, for example, if you can show that it was not reasonable for you to have claimed earlier. Alternatively, you may have been put off applying because you were given incorrect or misleading information in writing by a social security officer or Inland Revenue officer, or from an advice service such as a Citizens Advice Bureau, or a solicitor, accountant or doctor. If any of this applies to you, take advice.

In some cases you may be able to request backdating for more than three months, for example, if you claimed extra Income Support and were turned down because you were not receiving Disability Living Allowance (DLA). Once you successfully claim DLA, you can then ask the social security office to backdate your extra Income Support to the date you originally claimed it. Again, take advice.

With tax relief and tax allowances, you can claim for the previous six tax years if you qualified in any of these years.

8. You may be asked to attend a work-focused interview

At the time of writing the Government is piloting schemes that aim to ensure that benefit claimants are helped and encouraged into training or full-time work. These schemes are known as ONE in some areas, and Jobcentre Plus Pathfinders in other areas. If you live in a pilot area take advice, as you will be asked to attend what is called a work-focused interview at the Jobcentre Plus or local council offices to discuss how you could be helped into work or training if you claim any of the following: Income Support, Widowed Parent's Allowance, Bereavement Allowance, Incapacity Benefit, Invalid Care Allowance. In the Jobcentre Plus Pathfinders pilots, these benefits are also included: Industrial Injuries Disablement Benefit, Social Fund Payments and Maternity Allowance. The ONE pilots also include Housing Benefit and Council Tax Benefit.

If you are a single parent with children above a certain age and you claim Income Support, you have to attend a work-focused interview wherever you live - see *Income Support if you are pregnant or have children.*

9. You can claim for other people

With many forms of cash help, you can claim for other people as well as yourself - for example, your spouse (husband or wife) or your partner and any children you are responsible for - though usually you have to be living with them as well. The rules only allow you to claim for your partner if it is someone of the opposite sex you are living with as a couple. You cannot claim for a partner if you are in a gay or lesbian relationship with them - in that case you each have to claim in your own right.

10. And finally - tips on claiming

Details of how to claim are set out in each chapter, but here are a few extra tips.

- Fill in the claim form completely and legibly. Take advice if there is anything you are not clear about. Enclose all documentary evidence required, for example, medical certificates and bank statements. If any documents are missing, say so in a covering letter and send them on when you have them. Otherwise, if any queries arise the form will be sent back to you causing delays.

- In most cases you will have to include your National Insurance number (NINO) on the claim form and in any correspondence, not just for you but also for any other adult you are claiming for. If you don't know it, you will need to provide enough information to enable it to be traced (for example, previous employers, any previous names, previous addresses). If you or the other adult(s) have never had a NINO, you will need to enclose a form applying for one (the local social security office will provide you with a form).

- You may also be asked to provide further documents to confirm your identity, and that of other adults you are claiming for. This could be a birth certificate, a letter from the Home Office acknowledging your application for asylum, driving licence or passport, paid fuel or telephone bills, a council rent card. Take advice if you have none of these things.

- If you want to backdate your claim say so in a covering letter. You may have to give your reasons depending on the benefit - see above.

- Certain forms of cash help can be claimed in anticipation before you actually qualify - this is worth doing, as it should help you get paid on time when you do qualify. This applies to Council Tax Benefit, Disability Living Allowance, Attendance Allowance, Invalid Care Allowance, Retirement Pension, Income Based Job Seeker's Allowance, Contributory Based Job Seeker's Allowance, Income Support, Housing Benefit (in some circumstances - take advice), Guardian's Allowance, Working Tax Credit, Pension Tax Credit, and Child Tax Credit. These benefits have different rules on how far ahead of time you can claim - take advice.

- Make sure you send the claim form to the right address - take advice if you are unsure.

- If you want to amend your claim form you can write to ask for it back to do this, then resend it. If your letter arrives before a decision has been made, your claim will still be paid from the date it was originally received. You can also withdraw your claim but if a decision has already been made to pay you, you will still be paid up to the time you withdraw.

- Keep a copy of your claim form and any other papers you send in. You may need to refer to them later, for example, if the office loses your papers (that happens more frequently than it should!) or if you wish to appeal.

- Try to get the office to acknowledge your claim in writing so that you will have evidence of them receiving it and you can send a replacement straight away if they say they haven't had it.

- Budget for a delay. Different benefits take longer to be processed - eight weeks is common. Sometimes it is possible to get claims speeded up - see the chapters, get in touch with the office or take advice. You may have to use the complaints procedure for the office if the delay causes you major problems.

- Whatever the delay, many benefits payment should begin from the date the office received the claim (so you will receive the arrears with your first payment). However, this may not be the case with certain forms of cash help that you claim for in your Tax Return. Here you are usually claiming to be paid at the beginning of the next tax year (for example, tax allowances, tax reliefs or the new Working Tax Credit and Pension Tax Credit).
- With some benefits the payments may start from the date you phone or send in a request for a claim form, i.e. before you send in the claim form itself. Where this is the case, the chapter on that benefit will say so.

A-Z of benefits

Attendance Allowance

Are you aged 65 or over and are in poor health or disabled? You may be eligible for Attendance Allowance. It is not means-tested, there are two different rates depending on how much your need is, and it doesn't matter if you don't actually have anyone looking after you.

Qualification checklist

- You must have care needs, i.e. you need frequent attention with 'bodily functions', for example, washing, dressing, undressing and going to the toilet. The help may be needed through the night only, or the day, or night and day. Alternatively, you may need continual supervision to prevent you from putting yourself or others in danger.
- You must be aged over 65.
- You must not be receiving Disability Living Allowance.
- You must not be permanently in hospital or living in accommodation provided by or funded by a local authority. (If you are only in for part of any week, you may qualify for part payment for the days you are living out.)
- You have had these needs for the past six months at least.

NB If, in the opinion of your doctor, you are terminally ill, i.e. you are suffering from a progressive disease and you cannot reasonably be expected to live beyond the next six months, it is automatically assumed that you have care needs and it is not necessary for you to have had care or mobility needs for the past three months.

How to claim

See the chapter on *Disability Living Allowance* as the procedure and advice

Amount box

There are two rates of Attendance Allowance. Depending on how you are assessed, you will receive either the higher or lower rate.

Lower Rate
If you need frequent care throughout the day or during the night.
£37.65

Higher Rate
If you need frequent care throughout the day and during the night, or if you are terminally ill.
£56.25

on claiming and getting paid is the same. The only difference is that you will be paid for however long the Disability Benefits Centre estimates your needs may last for and there is no minimum period. It is not their policy to contact you randomly to check that you still qualify.

For further advice, the Benefits Enquiry Line run a telephone helpline which provides information on benefits for people with ill-health or disabilities, and carers (see *Useful addresses*).

Back to Work Bonus

This is a special payment you can claim if you have found a new job or increased your earnings and as a result have come off certain benefits.

Qualification checklist

- For at least 91 days, you or your partner have been entitled to Income Support or Income Based Job Seeker's Allowance. This is called the waiting period.
- Since the end of this waiting period, you or your partner have been receiving less Income Support or Income Based Job Seeker's Allowance because you've also been getting earnings from a part-time job (employed or self-employed). This is called the bonus period.
- You or your partner meet the 'work condition'; this means doing one of the following:
  - You have taken up a new job (or a paid job under the New Deal scheme).
  - You have returned to work.
  - You have increased your weekly hours of work to 16 or more.
  - You have increased your earnings so that you are no longer entitled to Income Based Job Seeker's Allowance or Income Support.
- If you were claiming Income Support, you will not qualify if you are within two days of your 60th birthday when you meet the work condition. If you were claiming Income Based Job Seeker's Allowance, you will not qualify if you are within two days of your 60th birthday if you are a woman, or your 65th birthday if you are a man.

- However, you can be excused meeting the work condition if you reached one of these birthdays while you were in a bonus period.

Amount box

In order to work out your bonus follow these four steps:

1. What were the earnings you or your partner received during the bonus period? Add up the total amount.

2. Were any of your earnings or other income ignored when the social security office worked out how much Income Support or Income Based Job Seeker's Allowance to pay you? Add up the total amount.

   If you are not sure what was ignored, the Appendix might help - *Income Support, Job Seeker's Allowance: Income Based, Minimum Income Guarantee and Disability Income Guarantee - the basics*. If you are still unsure, take advice.

3. Deduct your total at 2 from your total at 1 above,

4. Then divide what you have left by two. This will be the bonus, although the maximum you can usually get is £1,000.

As an example, let's presume that you have been claiming Job Seeker's Allowance continuously for six months and you have now taken a seven-hour per week job paying £34 per week. If you are single, the first £5 per week will be ignored so your Job Seeker's Allowance will be reduced by £29. If this job goes on for 24 weeks, then you will be able to increase your hours to 20 so you are no longer entitled to Job Seeker's Allowance (see Job Seeker's Allowance: Income Based). The 24 weeks will be your bonus period. Over this period, your £696 affected your Job Seeker's Allowance (£29 x 14) so your bonus will be half this = £348.

There are special rules on working out the bonus if you are a couple and you separate - take advice if this might affect you.

How to claim

Claim from your local Jobcentre Plus office - they will provide you with a form. A form is also obtainable from the DWP website at www.dwp.gov.uk. You can do this anytime from the week before the week in which your (or your partner's) Income Support or Job Seeker's Allowance ceases, until 12 weeks after it has ceased.

If you were on Income Support and you reach the age of 60, or on Income Based Job Seeker's Allowance and you reach 60 (woman) or 65 (man) during a bonus period, you should be paid any bonus due to you automatically.

Bereavement Allowance

This is a benefit paid to you if you have been widowed and you don't have children to look after. It has replaced Widow's Pension for anyone widowed after 9 April 2001.

Qualification checklist

- You are a widow or widower because your spouse died on or after 9 April 2001.
- You are under the age of 60 (widow) or 65 (widower).
- You were 45 or over when your spouse died.
- In their working life, up until death, your late spouse must have made sufficient National Insurance contributions in most of the tax years, either paid or credited.
- Despite saying above that credits count, there is still a need for your spouse to have had at least one tax year when he actually paid sufficient National Insurance contributions, although you can ignore this stipulation if he had been receiving long-term Incapacity Benefit in at least one of the two years before he died.
- These National Insurance requirements can be ignored if your spouse died as a result of an accident or disease directly or indirectly connected to work - see *Industrial Disablement Benefit.*
- You are not living with someone of the opposite sex as a partner.
- Normally you cannot qualify if you were criminally responsible for his death, but take advice as this is a complicated area.
- If your marriage was polygamous, you may not qualify, but take advice, as the law is complex on this. The same may apply if you were divorced in another country then remarried, as it is possible that the UK may not recognise your divorce.

How to claim

Claim from your local social security office. The procedure is the same as for Widowed Parent's Allowance. If you are entitled to Widowed Parent's Allowance, you will have to wait until your entitlement ceases (for example, when you stop getting Child Benefit for the children) before you receive Bereavement Allowance, as you cannot get the two benefits at once. If you do not qualify for Widowed Parent's Allowance, you will receive the Bereavement Allowance straight away. Be sure to claim within three months of qualifying as you cannot usually backdate any further than this.

Payment

You will get paid for 52 weeks, so long as you qualify as above but if you find a new partner, your benefit will be suspended. However, you can apply for it to be reinstated if you split up but not if you marry then separate!

Amount box

Your age when your spouse died	*Amount*
55 or over	£75.50
54	£70.22
53	£64.93
52	£59.65
51	£54.36
50	£49.08
49	£43.79
48	£38.51
47	£33.22
46	£27.94
45	£22.65

You may receive less than these amounts if your ex-spouse's National Insurance record is poor, but not poor enough for you not to qualify at all. However, you may be able to improve the record by making voluntary contributions – see *Retirement Pension: Category A* for how to do this.

Bereavement Payment

This is a one-off lump sum payment if you have been widowed.

Qualification checklist

- You are a widow or widower because your spouse died on or after 9 April 2001.

- If you are a widow whose spouse died before that date you may be able to make a late claim for widow's payment under an old scheme, but only if you didn't know about your spouse's death, or you couldn't prove it.
- Your late spouse had paid a certain minimum amount of National Insurance contributions in any tax year prior to his death. This qualification can be ignored if he died as a result of an accident or disease directly or indirectly connected to work – see *Industrial Disablement Benefit.*
- You were under 60 (woman) or 65 (man) when your spouse died. However, you can still qualify if you were older, but only if your spouse wasn't entitled to Category A Retirement Pension when he died, for example, he was under pensionable age.
- When your spouse died you weren't living with someone of the opposite sex as your partner.
- Normally you cannot qualify if you were criminally responsible for his death, but take advice as this is a complicated area.
- If your marriage was polygamous, you may not qualify, but take advice, as the law is complex on this. The same may apply if you were divorced in another country, then remarried, as it is possible that the UK may not recognise your divorce.

How to claim

You must claim within three months of the death, unless you were unaware of the death or you cannot prove that the death has occurred. Take advice. See *Widowed Parent's Allowance*, as the procedure for claiming is the same.

Amount box

The payment is a lump sum of £2,000.

Blind Person's Allowance - to reduce your Income Tax

This is a tax allowance you can claim if you are blind. You don't actually receive it but it reduces your tax bill. For further information, see *Appendix: Tax allowances and tax reliefs and your Tax Return - some general points.*

Qualification checklist

The following must apply to you:

- In England and Wales, you have to be registered as blind with the Social Services Department of your local council.
- In Scotland and Northern Ireland, you do not have to be registered and you will qualify if you cannot do work for which eyesight is essential.

Maximising the allowance

You can transfer all or part of the allowance to your spouse if you did not have enough income in the year to use up the allowance - see *Children's Tax Credit* as the procedure is the same.

How to claim

You have to submit a Tax Return to the Inland Revenue – see *Appendix: Tax allowances and tax reliefs and your Tax Return - some general points* for guidance on how to do this. On the Tax Return where it says local authority, put in the name of the council where you are registered blind, or write 'Scotland' or 'Northern Ireland' instead if you live there.

Amount box

Tax year ending 5 April 2003

The allowance is £1,450.

Care homes - help with the fees

If you, or someone you are close to, needs to go and live in a care home, for example, you may get help with the charges.

Qualification checklist

- You are assessed by your local council's Social Services Department as needing care in a care home, for example, because of your age or disability.
- Your capital is below £19,000 (or £18,500 in Scotland). Capital means any lump sum or one-off payment, savings and property. If the value of your capital is over this amount, it may be worth taking advice because some capital can be ignored so you could still qualify.

- If you own your property, the value of your home may be included as capital but not for the first 12 weeks of your stay or if you are only in the home temporarily (usually less than a year) and intend to return to it, or if it is up for sale and you want to use the proceeds to buy a more suitable property. If you are a joint owner, say with your spouse, then Social Services will only include a percentage of the value based on your 'share'. Take advice.
- Your income is below a certain amount. Most income counts, but some is ignored such as half of your personal or occupational pension if you pass at least this amount to your spouse. Also ignored are Child Benefit or child maintenance unless the child is staying with you. Housing costs, Attendance Allowance and Disability Living Allowance Care Component are ignored but only if your stay is temporary. Income on capital over £11,750 (£11,500 in Scotland) is counted on the basis of £1 per week for every £250. Although most of your income will have to be used to pay the charges, you will be entitled to a personal expenses allowance which you can keep back for your own needs. See *Amount box*.

Amount box

Some or all of your weekly charges may be met, if you qualify.

The personal expenses allowance you will be allowed is £16.80 per week.

In some cases this may be increased, for example, if you want to pursue a hobby or interest that is important to you, if you are taking time out of the home to stay with friends or family, or you are having to support a partner at home.

How to claim

You will need to apply to the Social Services Department for a needs assessment. If you are assessed as needing to live in a care home, they will find a suitable home for you - either in one of their own homes or an independent one. They will have a standard rate depending on the type of home.

Once you have had a needs assessment, apply to the Social Services Department for a financial assessment to decide whether you can have help to meet the home charges to cover your stay. You may be assessed as being able to afford to pay the charges yourself because you own a property. In this case, if you can't afford the charges because you haven't sold your property, Social Services will stop asking you to pay, but will place a legal charge on the property. This means they will automatically get their money back when the property is sold.

It is now possible to enter into what is called a written 'deferred payment' agreement which can continue in force until your death, but take advice on whether this is the best course of action for you.

Central Heating System Grant

You may be able to apply for a grant to pay to have central heating installed in your home. You will need to claim under the Home Energy Efficiency Scheme (HEES) under a scheme called Warm Front Plus, in England and HEES Plus, in Wales or Warm Deal, in Scotland.

Qualification checklist

- You must occupy the property for which the grant application is made and it must be your only residence, or your main one if you have other residences.
- You must either own or rent the property.
- You are 60 or over and you receive Income Support, Housing Benefit, Council Tax Benefit or Income Based Job Seeker's Allowance.
- In Wales only, you may also qualify if you are disabled or chronically sick and you receive Disabled Person's Tax Credit, Attendance Allowance, Disability Living Allowance, Industrial Injuries Disablement Benefit (if it includes Constant Attendance Allowance), War Disablement Pension (if it includes Constant Attendance Allowance or Mobility Allowance), or Income Support, Housing Benefit or Council Tax Benefit (if it includes a disability premium). You will also qualify if you look after a child under 16 who is receiving Disability Living Allowance.
- Also in Wales only, you may qualify if you are a single parent with a child under 16 where you receive Child Benefit and Income Support, Income Based Job Seeker's Allowance, Housing Benefit or Council Tax Benefit.

How to claim

See the chapter on *Home Insulation and Energy Efficiency Grants* as the procedure for claiming is the same. The bodies you should contact are the Home Energy Efficiency Scheme (HEES) in England and Wales or the Warm Deal in Scotland (see *Useful addresses*).

Grants awarded will be based on the cost up to a certain maximum. A central heating system will be provided on a lease but not if you are a council tenant. This means that if you are an owner-occupier, you will have to pay a charge to terminate the lease if you sell the property during the period covered by the lease. If you are a private tenant, your landlord will have to pay such a charge if they re-let the property to someone who would not have been eligible for a grant.

Child Benefit

Child Benefit is available to you if you are responsible for a child or children but this doesn't necessarily mean being their parent. You may qualify if you are an older sibling or other relative, adoptive parent, private foster parent or a step-parent.

Qualification checklist

- Your child is under 16, but in some circumstances under 19.
- The child must be living with you (they will count as living with you if they are sometimes away, for example, at boarding school or in residential accommodation due to ill-health or disability). If your child is sometimes away from home for other reasons, they may still qualify as living with you so long as in the past 16 weeks they haven't been away for more than 56 days.
- Alternatively, it is possible to qualify if you contribute to the maintenance of the child, so long as your payments are at least the amount of the Child Benefit itself.
- If you are not the only person who is claiming, your claim will be successful if you are regarded as higher in the order of priority than

Amount box

Eldest eligible child
£15.75

*Eldest eligible child - Lone Parent rate
£17.55

Other children
£10.55

* NB The rate for lone parents is not normally available to you if you claim after 5 July 1998, unless you have been on certain benefits such as a child addition to Widowed Mother's Allowance, or Invalid Care Allowance, or a pension, since before 6 July 1998. In that case, you may be able to make a new claim when you come off those benefits.

anyone else who claims. For example, if you live with the child, you will be seen as a higher priority than someone (say a separated parent) who made a claim because they maintained the child, so you will be allowed Child Benefit and they will not.

- However, even if you are lower in the order of priority than another person, you will still qualify if that person agrees that you should receive the payment. For example, if you are the child's father, your wife is deemed to be higher in the order of priority but she might agree that you can receive the benefit anyway, perhaps because she is working and you are staying at home to look after the children. (You will then qualify for Home Responsibilities Protection.)
- If you have an equal claim with someone else, for example, you are sharing care but are separated, the Child Benefit will still be paid to one of you. If you feel strongly that it should be split, you may be able to argue your case under the Human Rights Act. Take advice.
- If your child is married you will not qualify, unless they are separated or their spouse is in full-time education. If the child is living with a partner, you also will not qualify unless the partner is in full-time education.

How to claim

Get a claim form from the local social security office or the DWP website at www.dwp.gov.uk. Send the form to the Child Benefit Centre (see *Useful addresses*) enclosing a birth certificate, or an adoption certificate if applicable.

Payment

In order to work out how long your Child Benefit will be paid for, you need to know the compulsory school leaving age for your child. In England and Wales, this is the last Friday in June in the school year in which the child is 16. In Scotland, the date is different as it depends when your child's 16th birthday is.

- If your child leaves school before compulsory school leaving age, in England and Wales the benefit will continue until the first Monday in September. In Scotland, the benefit will continue until either the Sunday after the first Monday in January, the Sunday after the first Monday after Easter Monday, or the Sunday after the first Monday in September, whichever falls next after the compulsory school leaving age for the child.

- If your child leaves school after compulsory school leaving age but before reaching 16, the benefit will continue until whichever of the above dates comes next after his 16th birthday.

- If your child leaves school or college after compulsory school leaving age after 16 the benefit will continue until whichever of the above dates comes next after he leaves. However, so long as he remains at school or college you can continue to claim for him until his 19th birthday. Your child must remain in education full-time, which is at least 12 hours a week taught or supervised study and the education must be classed as 'non advanced', that is anything up to and including A-level.

However, if your child is under 18 and doesn't stay on in education there is a way you can extend your Child Benefit for up to 12 weeks. He has to be registered as available for work or on a training scheme such as Work-Based Learning for Young People, but not actually started on the scheme, and not in paid work for 24 hours or more, and not receiving Incapacity Benefit, Income Support or Income Based Job Seeker's Allowance.

Child Maintenance Bonus

This is a special payment you can claim if you receive child maintenance (or should receive it) and find a new job or increase your earnings so you must come off certain benefits.

Qualification checklist

- You are paid (or at least you are meant to be paid) child maintenance by someone else whilst you, or your partner, are receiving Income Support or Income Based Job Seeker's Allowance. This is called the bonus period.

- You, or your partner, meet what is called the work condition (for what this entails see *Back to Work Bonus*).

- Normally you will need to meet the work condition within 14 days of the end of the bonus period, but there are various exceptions to this, for example, if you are claiming when you come under the Child Support scheme new rules so take advice.

Amount box

The amount you receive is a lump sum which depends on the child maintenance you received (or should have received) during the bonus period above. How much child maintenance were you meant to be paid each week? If it was less than £5, you multiply that amount by the number of weeks in the bonus period. If it was £5 or more, you just multiply the number of weeks by £5. Remember that total. Now compare it with the actual amount of child maintenance you were paid over this period, the amount which affected your benefit. You will be paid whichever of these totals is the lower, but you cannot be paid more than £1,000.

For example, for 2 years (164 weeks) you should have been receiving £20 per week child maintenance but only received £3. Using the first method above, the total comes to £820 (164 x £5) Using the second method, the total is £492 (£3 x 164). The lower amount is £492 and this is lower than £1,000 so £492 is what you would receive.

If you and your partner each care for separate children for whom you receive maintenance, you can both claim the bonus, so you can each claim up to the £1,000 limit.

How to claim

Claim by completing a form provided by the local Jobcentre Plus office, also obtainable from the DWP website at www.dwp.gov.uk, and send it to that office. You can do this anytime from the week before the week in which your (or your partner's) Income Support or Job Seeker's Allowance ceases, until 28 days after it has ceased.

Child Tax Credit (CTC)

Believe it or not Child Tax Credit is a different benefit from Children's Tax Credit. However, this benefit will replace Children's Tax Credit from 7 April 2003. You can claim it if you are responsible for bringing up children whether you are a single parent, married or an unmarried couple. At the time of writing not all information on this benefit has been published, so if you have other queries, take advice.

Qualification checklist

You qualify if you meet the following criteria:

- You are bringing up a child or children under 16 (in order to qualify you usually have to be claiming Child Benefit for them).
- You can claim for children under 19 if they are in full-time non-advanced education (this is the same rule as for Child Benefit).
- You are aged 16 or over.
- Your income is below a certain amount, although your capital will have no effect on the Tax Credit, i.e. any lump sum or one-off payment, savings or property.

How to claim

If you are receiving either Working Families' Tax Credit, Disabled Person's Tax Credit or Children's Tax Credit, you should receive a letter from the Inland Revenue inviting you to claim in time to be paid from 7 April 2003. See *Working Tax Credit,* as the procedure for claiming and getting paid is the same. The exceptions are that both elements of CTC will normally be paid directly to the main carer of the children (usually the mother) and payment is likely to be made until 1 September following the child's 16th birthday (unless they are going on to further education).

Amount box

The maximum payments are:

- The individual element - to be paid per child - £10.48 for a baby under 1, £27.78 if aged 1- 16, or under 19 and in full time education.
- If the child is disabled - £41.44, and an extra £16.63 if the child is severely disabled.
- The family element - £10.48

To work out your actual entitlement add up the maximum you could get , then deduct from this your income. At least the first £13,230 of annual income is ignored, but more than this could also be ignored depending on the source of the income and your circumstances - take advice.

Children's Tax Credit

Despite its name, this is really another tax allowance, although you don't receive it as such but it reduces your tax bill. You can claim it if you are responsible for bringing up children whether you are a single parent, married or unmarried couple. For further information, see *Appendix: Tax allowances and tax reliefs and your Tax Return - some general points.* This tax credit is to be abolished in April 2003 and replaced with the (similarly named!) new Child Tax Credit.

Qualification checklist

You qualify if, during the previous tax year (that is the 12 months ending 5 April), the following categories applied to you:

- You were looking after a child or children (your own child, an adopted child or a stepchild). Any other child would count if you were meeting at least half of his maintenance costs.
- The child must be under 16 on 6 April at the beginning of the tax year.
- The child must have lived with you for at least part of the year.
- You cannot claim Married Couple's Allowance if you claim Children's Tax Credit, so you'll need to check out which of the two allowances you would be better off receiving.

Amount box

Tax year ending 5 April 2003

Maximum allowance, regardless of the number of children	£5,200
Maximum tax saving (as the allowance gives a 10% reduction to your tax bill)	£520

You won't get the full amount if you were not looking after the child throughout the year, or if someone else claims who also qualifies. You will also get less if you are a higher rate taxpayer - for every £3 of income taxed at the higher rate you lose £2 of the allowance. As an example, the higher tax rate kicks in if your income is greater than £29,900 *so if your income is £31,500, for example, that's £1,600 taxed at the higher rate, which means you lose £1,066 from the allowance (1,600 divided by 3, times 2).*

How to claim

In the first year you claim, you need to obtain the short claim form from one of the same places you can get a Tax Return (see *Appendix: Tax allowances and tax reliefs and your Tax Return - some general points*). After that, you claim for each year from the Inland Revenue in your Tax Return - see the above chapter for guidance on this. You can also get further help from the Children's Tax Credit Helpline (see *Useful addresses*).

There are rules on who in a couple can claim:

- If neither of you pays the higher tax rate, either of you can claim, or you can ask to share the credit between you. However, if you are the person with the lower income, the Inland Revenue will only accept your claim (even for a share) if the higher income person signs his agreement to this. If you are the higher earner, you do not need your partner's consent to receive all the credit! Usually, you will have to ask the tax office to make these changes before 6 April for the coming tax year, but there are exceptions so take advice.

- If either or both of you pay the higher tax rate, unfortunately you can only claim if you are the partner with the higher income and you will not be able to share or transfer the credit to the other partner. This is because higher tax rate payers get a reduced amount anyway (see above).

There are several situations where you may only be able to claim part of the credit. These are:

- If the child you are claiming for lives with someone else for part of the year, for example, a former partner or a grandparent, he may also want to claim the credit. You can decide between you if you want to share the credit and in what proportions. For example, you may decide with the other person that he looked after the child one third of the time, in which case in your Tax Return you can ask for the credit to be shared two thirds/one third between you and him. If you cannot reach an agreement, the Inland Revenue will make a decision for you.

- If the child you are claiming for is born during the tax year, you can only claim for the period after the birth, so if the child is born on 6 September, for example, you will qualify for the remaining six months of the year which means you'll claim 6/12 or one half of the credit.

- If you split from your spouse during the tax year, you have to look at the year in two parts. For the first part, you or your ex-partner will be claiming as per the rules above. For the second part, you will be claiming in accordance with your new circumstances and perhaps sharing the credit with your ex-partner if they still qualify. In order to work out your total claim, you will have to calculate the proportion of each part of the year in days.

  For example if you split up on 4 August, you will have had 121 days as a couple and 244 days separated. The 121 days as a proportion of the year is 121/365. Remember, the whole credit is £5,200 so this proportion will be £1,724. This will leave £3,476 available for the rest of the year which you may qualify for.

- If you move in with someone who already has a child during the tax year, you may be able to claim a share of the tax credit with that person but you can only claim for the proportion of the tax year you were looking after the child. Work out your proportion as above.

Maximising the allowance

If you do not have enough income in the year to use up the allowance, and you have a partner with whom you have lived for at least some of the tax year, you can transfer your unused tax allowance to him. This is worth doing if he himself has tax to pay. It does not matter whether or not you are married to your partner. You can simply request the transfer of any surplus in your Tax Return and it will be deducted from your partner's tax bill. You can, if it suits you, wait up to five years and ten months after the end of the tax year to have this transfer made. Alternatively, if you know in advance that you're not going to have enough income to benefit from the allowance, and your spouse is an employee, you can ask the Inland Revenue to transfer the part you think will be unused to your spouse's tax coding.

Christmas Bonus

You may be entitled to a small payment at Christmas.

Qualification checklist

You qualify if you are entitled to one of the following benefits in the week beginning with the first Monday in December:

- Attendance Allowance
- Constant Attendance Allowance
- Disability Living Allowance
- Incapacity Benefit at the long-term rate
- Income Support (from age 65 (man) and 60 (woman))
- Invalid Care Allowance
- Mobility Supplement (as part of War Disablement Pension)
- Retirement Pension
- Unemployability Supplement (as part of War Disablement Pension)

- War Disablement Pension (if aged 65)
- War Widow's Pension
- Widow's Pension
- Widowed Mother's Allowance
- Widowed Parent's Allowance

You will also be eligible if you receive Industrial Death Benefit or Severe Disablement Allowance (note that it is not now possible to make a new claim for these two benefits so they are not mentioned in this book).

- If you are a war disablement pensioner who gets none of these benefits, you will still qualify if you are 65 or over.

Amount box

You will receive a payment of £10.

If you are a couple, you may claim an extra £10 for your partner or spouse if he is not entitled in his own right, but only if you are both over pension age (60 for a woman, 65 for a man) by the end of that week in December. In this case, you must be getting Income Support only or failing that you are entitled to an adult dependant increase of the listed benefits for that person.

- If you are a couple, you may both qualify in your own right - see *Amount box.*

How to claim

Normally you are automatically paid the bonus if you qualify, but if you miss out, contact your social security office.

Payment

You are paid as an extra amount on top of your other benefit payment.

Cold weather payments

You may be able to receive money to help with fuel costs if the weather is especially cold.

Qualification checklist

The following must apply to you:

- You are receiving (or about to receive) Income Support or Income Based Job Seeker's Allowance for at least one day during the period of cold weather.

- You have a child under 5 in your family or included in your benefit is one of these premiums: disability, severe disability, disabled child, pensioner, higher pensioner or enhanced pensioner premiums.
- You live in a postcode area where the weather station forecasts or records state an average daily temperature of 0 degrees centigrade or less for seven consecutive days. (This information will be automatically collected by the DWP.)

How to claim

The payment should be made automatically. However, if this doesn't happen, you should contact your local social security office. You should know when you are due a payment as the social security office will advertise and distribute posters and leaflets. You will be sent a cheque for each week of cold weather.

Amount box

You will receive £8.50 for each week of cold weather.

Community Care Grant

You may be eligible for a grant to meet certain costs such as travel expenses or essential repair costs. You do not have the right to receive it, it is discretionary, but you should certainly apply if your circumstances fit.

Qualification checklist

- You are receiving Income Support or Income Based Job Seeker's Allowance when you apply. The only exception to this would be if, within the next six weeks, you are leaving institutional or residential care (say prison, hospital, care home, hostel, supported housing, foster home or any place where you receive a substantial amount of care). Then you may qualify if it is likely that when you leave you'll be claiming Income Support or Income Based Job Seeker's Allowance.
- You do not have too much capital - see *Amount box.*
- You must need the grant either to help you settle in the community after you leave institutional or residential care above, or to help you stay in the community rather than having to enter institutional or residential care.

- You may also qualify if you or your family living with you are facing a lot of extra financial pressure, for example, you are moving home, or you are victim of a disaster, or you have high repair bills, or you need to carry out structural repairs to keep your home habitable, or you have high clothing and washing costs because you have a disabled child.
- Also, you may be covered if you have been homeless and you are setting up home as part of a planned programme that has been organised for you.
- You may qualify to claim travel expenses and overnight accommodation to visit an ill relative or attend a relative's funeral, to move home, or to ease a domestic crisis.
- Because the grant is discretionary, there may be expenses in other situations that you can apply for, but some expenses are definitely not allowed such as most costs related to education, employment and medical treatment. Do take advice.

Amount box

The amount you request, if approved, will be met provided this is regarded as reasonable.

The minimum payment is £30 - there is no maximum.

Your grant will be reduced if you have capital over £500 (or £1,000 if you or your partner are 60 or over). The reduction will be the actual amount of the savings, so if, for example, your grant was worked out as £970 and you had £700 savings, you would end up with £270 (£970 - £700).

How to claim

You need form SF300, available from your social security office or from the DWP website at www.dwp.org.uk. You will need to supply evidence of any expenses incurred and your circumstances. Make sure that you claim for all the help you need; give the cost of each item and be specific about why you need the items, for example, for a carpet or bedding say which room they are to be for. Also say how - for each major item applied for - getting a grant would improve your circumstances and fulfil the purpose intended (for example, to help you avoid having to go into care).

The social security office will first assess the merits of your application, and then he will see what priority the application falls into in your case. It could be that he decides that you fit the criteria for a grant but you are low priority. This may mean that there is not enough money in the budget to pay you. There are national guidelines on the priority levels but each local office is able to use its own guidance within this framework. If your application is approved, a decision is then made on whether the money you are claiming is reasonable, maybe by comparing with trade prices.

After considering your application, the social security office may decide to offer you a loan instead - a budgeting loan, or even a crisis loan (see *In brief*). You can of course refuse this if you wish.

You are paid by Giro cheque, but in some cases the supplier of an item you are applying for may be paid directly.

Council Tax Benefit

Do you dread having to pay that Council Tax bill? Perhaps you qualify for Council Tax Benefit. This is a means-tested benefit, administered by your local council's Housing Benefit department.

Qualification checklist

The following conditions must apply to you:

- You are legally liable to pay the Council Tax on the property (or at least jointly liable with someone else). This will mean that you usually live in the property as your home.
- If you are jointly liable with a partner or spouse, only one of you can claim.
- You are aged 18 or over (as you cannot be liable for Council Tax if you're under 18 anyway!).
- You must have income and capital below a certain amount (see *Amount box*). The rules on this are the same as for Housing Benefit.

How to claim

You claim from your local council - the procedure is the same as for Housing Benefit. You can claim up to eight weeks before you receive a Council Tax bill. If you've paid your bill in advance before you claim that's OK, but usually you will only be awarded benefit, if you qualify, from the date the council received your claim. However, there

Amount box

The council first works out the maximum Council Tax Benefit available to you. This is usually done by dividing up your total bill for the year into 52 weeks.

However, if you have other people (called non-dependants) living in your home, such as an adult son or daughter, or grandmother, a deduction will be made from this weekly figure before arriving at your maximum. This amount will depend on their earnings.

A deduction will also be made if you live in a home valued in one of the higher Council Tax bands. Then, a funny little formula applies. If your home is band F, your maximum benefit will be 11 thirteenths of your weekly Council Tax; if your home is band G, it is 11 fifteenths; and if you're in band H, it is 11 eighteenths. So, if you live in a band G property and you pay £930 per year Council Tax, weekly this works out at £17.80. To find out 11 fifteenths, divide by 15 (= £1.19) and multiply by 11 = £13.07 which will be your maximum Council Tax.

Once the maximum figure in your case is arrived at, if you are claiming Income Support or Income Based Job Seeker's Allowance, you will then be allowed this amount in full.

Otherwise, the amount of benefit you will actually get, up to the maximum, will be based on what is called your applicable amount. This can be worked out by totalling up all the elements that might apply to you in the Amount box in the chapter *Appendix: Income Support, Job Seeker's Allowance: Income Based, Minimum Income Guarantee and Disability Income Guarantee – the basics*. These elements make up what is called your 'applicable amount'.

If your income is less than, or equal to, your applicable amount, then you will get the maximum Council Tax Benefit available to you. If, on the other hand, your income is greater than your applicable amount, the amount of benefit you will get (if any) will be the maximum benefit minus 20% of the difference between your income and the applicable amount.

So, for example, if your maximum Council Tax is worked out as £13.07 per week, and you are claiming as a couple, your applicable amount is £84.65. Say if your income is £140 per week (after ignored income is taken off), this leaves a difference of £55.35. 20% of this difference is £11.07. The benefit you will receive is therefore the £13.07 maximum minus this £11.07, which comes to £2 per week.

is a special rule on backdating if your council hasn't set a Council Tax rate by the start of the financial year. In this case, so long as you claim within four weeks of the rate being announced, your claim will be backdated to the start of the year.

Payment

Payment is usually made as a reduction in your Council Tax bill, but if you've already paid, you will need to ask for the benefit to be paid directly to you. Should you not do so, you may find that it is held back and credited towards next year's bill. If you have a joint bill with someone other than a spouse or partner, any benefit he receives will be credited on your bill as well as his, and vice versa.

The rules on how long your benefit will last, renewals, change of circumstances are the same as for Housing Benefit.

Council Tax Benefit (Extended payments)

This benefit is to help you with your Council Tax if you've just started a new job or increased your hours and as a result will be coming off certain benefits.

Qualification checklist

- You must be starting a job (including self-employment) for 16 or more hours per week or you are increasing your hours to that amount; or
- Your partner (if any) started a job of 24 hours or more per week or increased his hours to that amount, or
- You qualify for Lone Parent Run On (see *Lone Parent Run On*).

Also,

- In either case, you must expect the job to last at least five weeks.
- You or your partner have been getting Income Support or Income Based Job Seeker's Allowance (or equivalent) for at least the last 26 weeks prior to the new job or extra hours.
- Any income you receive, or any capital you have, is ignored.

How to claim

You have to tell the Jobcentre and the council that you have increased your hours or taken a new job. Do this within four weeks of the change or you could miss out. Your Council Tax bill should be reduced by the council. If not, do get in touch with them.

> **Amount box**
>
> The weekly amount paid is usually the actual Council Tax Benefit you were getting in your last full week of being on Income Support or Income Based Job Seeker's Allowance.

Payment

Payment is for the first four weeks of your new job or extra hours or, if you qualify for Lone Parent Run On, for the two weeks after that ends.

Of course, you can still claim ordinary Council Tax Benefit as a result of the new job or extra hours (see *Council Tax Benefit*). If you qualify for the same period as the Extended Council Tax Benefit, you'll receive whichever is the higher for those four weeks.

Council Tax: Second Adult Rebate

This benefit is to help you pay your Council Tax bill. It is an alternative type of Council Tax Benefit that can be paid instead of, but not as well as, Council Tax Benefit.

Qualification checklist

The following conditions must apply to you:

- You are legally liable to pay the Council Tax on the property (or at least jointly liable with someone else). This will mean that you usually live in the property as your home.
- You are aged 18 or over (as you can't be liable for Council Tax under 18 anyway!).
- No-one living in your home pays you rent, although there are some exceptions to this such as full-time students, so take advice.
- You have one or more people living with you who are classed as 'second adults'. This is defined as someone living with you as a guest, maybe a relative or in-law, or adult son or daughter or friend, but it cannot be a full-time student, or a

partner or spouse; or someone else who is jointly liable to pay Council Tax with you.

- If you are claiming as a couple, no-one living with you can usually count as a second adult, although there are a few exceptions such as if you are both full-time students. Take advice.
- Also, the second adult(s) can only enable you to qualify if his income is low enough. See *Amount box.*

How to claim

Claim from your local council using the same forms and procedures as Council Tax Benefit. The council are obliged to consider you for both benefits at the same time. If you qualify for both, they should pay you the one you would be better off on. If you have doubts about whether this has happened, take advice.

Amount box

1. In order to work out your entitlement, the council firstly takes your weekly Council Tax liability and deducts from this any discount you may be entitled to (including for disability) - see *In brief.* A deduction may also be made in the same way as for Council Tax Benefit if you live in a high tax band.
2. Secondly, the council works out what percentage of your bill can be discounted. This depends on the second adult's income. If he is on Income Support or Income Based Job Seeker's Allowance, you will get a 25% discount. If his income is up to £133 per week, you will get 15%; if it is £131 to £169.99, you get 7.5%; and if it is more than £170, no discount at all. The rules for what counts as income are a bit different to other benefits, for example, if the second adult is on Income Support or Income Based Job Seeker's Allowance and he works part-time, that income is all ignored and any Attendance Allowance or Disability Living Allowance is also ignored.
3. If you are jointly liable for the Council Tax with someone else (not your spouse or partner), you will only get a Second Adult Rebate for your share. For example, if you are a tenant sharing with two other joint tenants, you will get one third of the rebate.

NB If you live alone, you can claim a 25 per cent reduction on your Council Tax. *See In Brief.*

Disability Income Guarantee

This is the name the Government now gives to your Income Support if you or your partner are severely disabled.

Qualification checklist

Firstly, see *Appendix: Income Support, Job Seeker's Allowance: Income Based, Minimum Income Guarantee* and *Disability Income Guarantee - the basics* as you must meet all the conditions set out in the Qualification checklist in that chapter.

Secondly, to qualify you or your partner must be entitled to the highest rate care component of Disability Living Allowance.

How to claim

For information on how to claim and how you are paid, see *Income Support if you are pregnant or have children* as the procedure is the same. The Benefits Enquiry Line (see *Useful addresses*) can give you further information.

Amount box

In order to work out your entitlement, see *Appendix: Income Support, Job Seeker's Allowance: Income Based, Minimum Income Guarantee and Disability Income Guarantee - the basics.*

Also, if you have a mortgage, see *Mortgage and other loans - help with repayments.*

Disability Living Allowance (DLA)

Do you need care or help with getting around, at least some of the time, because you have a disability? Disability Living Allowance is not means-tested, and not affected if you have a job. It is paid at different rates depending on the assessment of your needs, and it doesn't matter if you don't actually have anyone looking after you.

Qualification checklist

- You have either care or mobility needs (or both).
- You must be under 65 when you first claim (but if you are still receiving DLA for care needs which you applied for before you were 65 and your health deteriorates, you can ask for your claim to be reviewed after 65).

- You can claim for a child from the age of 3 months if you are claiming for care needs, but the child must be at least three years old if you are claiming for mobility needs.
- It would benefit you to take trips outdoors every so often.
- You are not permanently in hospital or living in accommodation provided by or funded by a local authority (if you are only in for part of any week, you may qualify for part payment for the days you are living out).
- You have had these needs for the past three months at least and you will be likely to have these needs for the next six months.

NB If, in the opinion of your doctor, you are terminally ill, i.e. you are suffering from a progressive disease and you cannot reasonably be expected to live beyond the next six months, it is automatically assumed that you have care needs and it is not necessary for you to have had care or mobility needs for the past three months.

So what are care needs?

You will be deemed to have care needs if at least one of the following applies to you:

- You need some help at least with 'bodily functions', during the day, or the night, or both. For example, eating, washing, dressing and undressing and going to the toilet. This can also include help which enables someone to take part in social activities.
- You need supervision to prevent you from being a danger to yourself or others.
- Only applicable if you are over the age of 16: Your disability prevents you from preparing and cooking a main meal, although you have all the ingredients (for example, peeling or chopping vegetables, coping with hot or heavy pans, lifting, carrying, bending, etc.). You will not qualify under this point just because you are a 'can't cook - won't cook' person. You do have to demonstrate that your disability or illness prevents you from doing these tasks.

And mobility needs...?

In order to have mobility needs, at least one of the following must apply:

- You cannot walk outdoors or go on an unfamiliar route without guidance or supervision from another person most of the time. There could be all sorts of reasons for this, for example, you are blind, or profoundly deaf, or liable to have panic attacks.
- You are unable to walk at all.
- You can walk but doing so outdoors is very difficult for you, for example, you can only get along by walking very slowly, or it causes you pain, discomfort or breathlessness after walking a certain distance, or bad weather makes things difficult for you.
- The exertion of walking is likely to cause serious deterioration to your health.
- You have no legs or feet or at least you are without the use of them.
- You are blind and deaf and need someone to help you get about out of doors.
- You have severe learning difficulties and can behave very disruptively.

NB If you are claiming for a child under the age of 16, you also have to show that he needs more attention or supervision than normal for a child of that age. Take advice on this.

How to claim

You can get a date stamped claim form by telephoning the Benefits Enquiry Line (see *Useful addresses*), or by obtaining a claim pack from the Disability Benefits Unit (DBU) by completing the tear-off coupon from leaflet DS704, available from post offices, social security offices or some advice services. Ask for form DLA1 for an adult, and DLA 1 (child) for a child under 16. You will have six weeks from the date stamp to return the claim form by post to the DBU for your area. If you do so, you will be paid from that date (if you qualify!).

Alternatively, you can obtain the forms from the website www.dwp.gov.uk, in which case you will be paid from the date the claim is received.

Section 2 of the form asks for details of how your disability or ill-health affects you. Do be realistic with your answers as it is easy to underestimate your needs or to forget to say certain things because you have got used to managing. For example, how long would it take you to get dressed on your own, and do you need someone nearby if you have to get up in the night in case you have a fall? You can telephone the DBU for help and in some cases they may agree to visit you to help you to apply.

Part of Sections 1 and 2 have to be completed by someone who knows you or your circumstances well enough to confirm your illness or disability and the effects it has on you. Ask a carer, a social worker or your GP (you should not be charged) or a friend or relative will do. Send the form in anyway if you cannot get this section completed, as the social security office will arrange this for you if necessary.

Before a decision is reached on whether you qualify, and at what rate, the person above may be contacted, or perhaps your GP. You may also be asked to attend a medical examination.

If you are terminally ill and claiming for care needs, no medical will be required. Your claim will be dealt with under 'special rules', and should be decided within 15 days. You will not have to fill in the parts of the claim form relating to your personal care needs; instead you will need to provide form DS1500, completed by your GP or consultant, detailing your medical condition. You will still need to fill in the information required about your mobility needs if you have any. You are allowed to claim on behalf of someone who is terminally ill without them knowing.

Payment

If you are in hospital or residential accommodation for part of the week, you will be paid only for the days you are living out. This could be just one or two days a

Amount box

There are two components of Disability Living Allowance. The care component is for care needs and the mobility component is for mobility needs. Depending on how you are assessed, you will receive either one or both components at one of the rates below.

CARE COMPONENT

Lower Rate

Your disability prevents you from cooking a main meal or you need care for part of the day. £14.90

Middle Rate

If you need frequent care throughout the day or during the night. £37.65

Higher Rate

If you need frequent care throughout the day and during the night, or if you are terminally ill. £56.25

MOBILITY COMPONENT

Lower

If you cannot walk outdoors without guidance or supervision most of the time. £14.90

High

If you have any of the other problems listed above in this chapter in getting about. £39.30

week. If you receive higher rate mobility, you can hire or purchase a car or electric wheelchair under the Motability scheme (see *In brief*). If you do so, your benefit will be paid directly to the scheme.

You will be paid for however long the Disability Benefits Unit estimates your needs may last for. This could be indefinitely or for a fixed period (minimum six months). In the case of a fixed period, you will be invited to make a renewal claim six months before the award runs out. if you are not reminded, do contact the Disability Benefit Unit. If you qualified before you reached 65, you can continue to receive DLA after you reach this age, so if you're coming up to 65 and you think you might qualify, it is likely to be to your advantage to claim now!

However, if you have a change of circumstances that might affect your entitlement, you should report these to the Unit. If your health has improved, they may lower the rate you qualify for (see *Amount box*) or stop your DLA altogether. If your health has deteriorated, you may qualify for one of the higher rates. During the time you are receiving DLA you may be randomly contacted by post or personal visit to fill in a questionnaire to check that you still qualify. You may also have to have another medical. This should not happen if you have a fixed period award for less than three years, or if you are severely disabled.

For further advice, the Benefits Enquiry Line run a telephone helpline which provides information on benefits for people with ill-health or disabilities, and carers (see *Disabled Person's Tax Credit*).

Disabled Facilities Grant

If you have a disability, you may want to make changes in your home in order to make day-to-day living easier.

Qualification checklist

- Usually you must be living in the property as an owner-occupier or tenant (a private or a council tenant).
- You are physically or mentally disabled because of illness or injury, or you have substantially impaired sight, hearing or speech. This may mean you are registered, or could be registered, with the Social Services Department of your council but this is not essential.

- Your income is below a certain amount. The assessment is the same as for a Renovation Grant except that only you, if you are the disabled person, and your partner can be subjected to the means test, not anyone else living with you. The exception will be if the disabled person is a child, in which case the income of the parent(s) will be assessed.
- If you are a landlord, you can also apply for a grant if you own the property and you let it out or intend to let it out to a disabled tenant - take advice.

What can be claimed for?

A Renovation Grant can be paid to do the following:

- Make it easier for you to get access to your home, and rooms within.
- Make your home safe for you and anyone living with you.
- Enable you to have easily accessible and usable bathroom and kitchen facilities.
- Improve or replace your heating system to meet your needs.
- Make it easier for you to use power supplies, for example, for lighting and heating.
- Make it easier for you to move around the house to care for a dependant such as a child.
- Your local council have the discretion to make other grants available, for example, for adaptations which make your life at home easier.

How to claim

Claim from your local council. The procedure for claiming and payment is mostly the same as for a House Renovation Grant. You will usually have to sign a declaration that you will live in the property for at least five years after the works are completed, but exceptions will be made for health or other special reasons. The council have to decide whether the works proposed are necessary and appropriate for your needs as a disabled person and reasonable and practicable in relation to the property. They may seek the

Amount box

See the chapter on *House Renovation Grant*, as the amount is worked out in the same way. The maximum mandatory grant you can get is £25,000 (£24,000 in Wales) but your local council have the discretion to pay more than this if they think it is needed.

opinion of the Social Services Department of the council, and may even ask you to apply for an occupational therapy assessment before they will consider your claim. However, they are not allowed to stop you claiming if you want to do that before any assessment.

Disabled Person's Tax Credit (DPTC)

Is your earning power restricted because you have a disability or ill-health? This benefit may help to top up your earnings and if you have children, you may get help with childcare expenses as well. Any claim you make now will be paid until 6 April 2003 as the benefit will be replaced from that date by the Working Tax Credit .

Qualification checklist

- You work on average 16 or more hours per week, your average income is below a certain amount (see *Amount box*) and your capital is not more than £8,000. All these conditions are the same as for Working Families' Tax Credit.

- You have a physical or mental disability that puts you at a disadvantage in getting a job or you develop a disability that leads to your earnings from your current employment being reduced.

- You are currently receiving Disability Living Allowance or Attendance Allowance, or you have an invalid vehicle, or you receive Industrial Disablement Benefit or a War Disablement Pension and that includes a special increase for your attendance needs.

- You can also qualify if, for at least one or more days in the 26 weeks prior to your claim, you were getting the higher rate of short-term Incapacity Benefit or long-term Incapacity Benefit or Severe Disability Allowance. Alternatively, you qualify if for one or more days in the 26 weeks prior to your claim you received Income Support, Income Based Job Seeker's Allowance, Housing Benefit or Council Tax Benefit but only if your entitlement included a disability or a higher pension premium.

- If you became disabled whilst you were employed, you may qualify even without having been on these benefits. Firstly, you must receive either Statutory Sick Pay, the lower rate of short-term Incapacity Benefit, or Income Support because of your illness or disability. Failing that, you must have been allowed National Insurance credits for up to 20 weeks of illness or disability ending within

Amount box

Your entitlement will be made up of different individual tax credits depending on your circumstances.

- If you are a single person without a child and your income is less than £73.50 (called the 'applicable amount'), you will receive the maximum DPTC. If you live with a partner or spouse, your combined income will have to be less than £94.50. If you are a single parent the figure is also £94.50. In order to work out what the maximum DPTC will be for you, just add together the credits in this box that apply to you.
- If your income is more than the amounts above, work out your entitlement by adding together the credits that apply to you and then from this total deduct 55% of the excess. For example, say you are a single person and you calculate that your maximum entitlement is £62.10 and your income is £105.00 per week, this is £31.50 greater than your 'applicable amount'. 55% of this £31.50 is £17.32, so you'll need to deduct £17.32 from the maximum entitlement = £44.78. This will be your entitlement.

Most of the actual amounts of the credits are the same as for Working Families' Tax Credit - see the *Amount box* in the chapter on this benefit.

There is, however, one extra credit which is:

If you are single without a child	£62.10

the eight weeks before you claim. Secondly, a doctor must certify that, in his opinion, your disability will continue for at least six months. Thirdly, due to your disability, your earnings are expected to be at least 20 per cent lower than they would otherwise have been. This has to mean a minimum reduction of £15.

NB You are not allowed to receive DPTC and Working Families' Tax Credit at the same time.

Making a claim

You claim DPTC on form DPTC 1, available from the Tax Credit office, Inland Revenue Enquiry Offices or your local social security office. The procedure and guidance are the same as for Working Families' Tax Credit. You can ask your local social security office to complete the form for you and they can then arrange for your claim to be speeded up. Also you can apply through the Benefits Enquiry Line over the phone. When they have completed your claim form they will send it to you to sign.

When you are claiming for the first time, you have to sign a declaration that your disability puts you at a disadvantage in getting a job. With a renewal claim you may have to complete a longer self-assessment form as well, and give names of two medical professionals who know about your situation. The Tax Credit Office may check with them to confirm your answers to the questions. You will not usually be asked to attend a medical examination.

The arrangements for getting paid, and getting further information, are the same as for Working Families' Tax Credit (see the chapter on this benefit) except the helpline number is different.

For further advice, contact the Tax Credit Office or the Benefits Enquiry Line (see *Useful addresses*).

Employee expenses: tax relief

You may qualify for tax relief on certain expenses you incur as a result of doing your job as an employee. This may mean you will have less tax to pay. For more information on tax reliefs and how to claim them, see *Appendix: Tax allowances and tax reliefs and your Tax Return - some general points.*

Qualification checklist

- The general Inland Revenue rule is that you can claim tax relief on expenses which are 'spent wholly, exclusively and necessarily' in doing your job.
- Of course, you cannot claim for expenses your employer has wholly reimbursed, but if they have only partly reimbursed you, you may be able to claim for the balance.
- There is no definitive list of what qualifies and what doesn't under these rules. If you think it should qualify then claim it, but your tax office will decide based on the information you give them. The following is guidance:
    - You can claim for mileage on journeys carried out in the course of your job, but not usually travel between home and work. However, you can claim if you are travelling to a temporary workplace, if you are going

there for a limited time or a temporary purpose. You can also claim if you job involves a great deal of travel and you do not have one permanent workplace. Take advice.

- If you are claiming for travel expenses, you can also claim relief for meals and accommodation costs (subsistence) incurred in making the journey, even expenses like phone calls if they were to the office not home!

- You can claim for fees or subscriptions you have to pay as a condition of your job (such as professional fees).

How to claim

Claim the relief by entering the amount of the expenses in the Employment Supplementary pages of the Tax Return under the various headings such as 'travel and subsistence costs' or 'professional fees and subscriptions'.

To claim mileage costs if you are driving, you have to use the Inland Revenue rules on mileage allowances depending on the car's engine capacity. Take advice.

Funeral expenses payment

Paying for a funeral can blow a big hole in your budget but there is a scheme which may help you meet these costs.

Qualification checklist

- You, or your partner, have accepted responsibility for paying the funeral expenses.

- You or your partner are receiving or about to receive Income Support, Income Based Job Seeker's Allowance, Hardship Payments, Housing Benefit, Council Tax Benefit, Council Tax Second Adult Rebate, Working Families' Tax Credit or Disabled Person's Tax Credit.

- The deceased person must have been your partner when he died, or your child, for whom you were responsible when he died. However, if you are living apart from the child's other parent, that parent would have to be receiving one of the above benefits as well (except in the case of a stillbirth).

Amount box

The following expenses will be met if regarded as reasonable:

- Cost of purchasing a new burial plot and burial fees (but not fees for burying ashes).
- Cremation fees, including medical documentation and fee for removing a pacemaker.
- Cost of papers needed to release the deceased's assets.
- Funeral transport costs in excess of £50.
- Travel expenses for a return journey to enable you to organise the funeral.
- Up to £600 for any other expenses such as funeral director's fees, religious costs and flowers.

However, before you are paid the following will be deducted:

- Any of the deceased's assets available to you before probate (or letters of administration if there was no will).
- Any lump sum legally due to you or a member of your family on the death of the deceased, for example, from an insurance policy, burial club or occupational pension scheme.
- Any contribution to funeral expenses paid by a relative or charity (but not all trusts, for example, payments from the Macfarlane Trust (see *In Brief*) are ignored), or a funeral grant paid to a war disablement pensioner.
- Any amount due under a prepaid funeral plan.

- Otherwise, you may qualify under special rules as a close relative or close friend of the deceased. You would have to have been in close contact with him when he was alive so take advice. If the deceased had a partner, parent, son or daughter with whom he was still in touch, or if he had another close relative or friend in closer contact than you, you may not qualify.
- If the deceased dies in hospital and you do not take responsibility for the funeral because of low income, then the hospital is obliged to pay for a basic funeral. If

the death occurred elsewhere and you cannot afford the funeral, the local council will make the necessary arrangements.

How to claim

Claim on form SF200, available from your local social security office or from the DWP website at www.dwp.org.uk. You will need to supply evidence of the expenses incurred and your circumstances. This will have to include others such as any partner and (in the case of a child) their other parent if this isn't your partner.

Payment

You are paid by Giro cheque. Any expenses incurred by the funeral director are paid directly to them unless you have already paid the bill. Any payments made can be recovered from the deceased's estate, if there is one, as a priority over anything else.

War pensioners

If the deceased was a war pensioner a non-means-tested grant can be claimed from the Veterans Agency instead of the above. This is for people who were entitled to a War Disablement Pension or the related allowances (see *War Disablement Pension and other allowances*) and who died as a result of service in the armed forces, or whilst being treated for their pensioned war disablement.

Guardian's Allowance

You can claim Guardian's Allowance if you are looking after a child whose parents are not around, for example, if you are a step-parent or a guardian.

Qualification checklist

- Normally you must be eligible for Child Benefit for the child, although in some cases you may still qualify, for example, where you don't get Child Benefit yourself but you live with your partner and he gets it.

Also one of the following must apply:

- Both the child's parents are dead.
- One parent is dead and the other cannot be traced.

- The child's parents never married and the mother is dead and the father does not have parental responsibility.
- The child's parents never married and the mother is dead and the father is unknown.
- The surviving parent is in prison and has at least another five years to serve.

Amount box

Full rate	£11.35 per child
Reduced rate	£9.65

You can get the reduced rate for a child if you are getting the higher rate of Child Benefit for that child (see *Child Benefit*).

- The parents are divorced, one parent is dead and that parent had a residence order for the child, and the other parent is not paying maintenance for the child.

NB If the child is adopted, it will be the adopted parents who count as parents above, not the natural parents.

How to claim

Claim on form BG1, available from the local social security office or the DWP website at www.dwp.gov.uk. You will also need a birth certificate if this is available. Send your claim form to the Guardian's Allowance Unit.

Hardship payments if you are unemployed

In some cases, if you fail to qualify for Income Based Job Seeker's Allowance (JSA) and therefore you have little or no money to live on, you may be able to claim a hardship payment.

Qualification checklist

Firstly, one of the following must apply to you:

- You have just claimed Job Seeker's Allowance and you are waiting for a decision as to whether you satisfy the labour market conditions (see page 81).
- You do not qualify for Job Seeker's Allowance because you do not satisfy the labour market conditions.

- Your Job Seeker's Allowance is suspended because the Jobcentre have some doubt about whether you continue to satisfy the labour market conditions.
- Your Job Seeker's Allowance has been suspended or stopped (see *Job Seeker's Allowance: Contribution Based*).

Secondly, you only qualify if all these points apply:

- You (or your partner) do not qualify for Income Support.
- You would otherwise qualify for Income Based Job Seeker's Allowance.
- You can satisfy the Jobcentre that you or your partner will suffer hardship if you are not paid. This will be easier if one of the following applies to you or your partner (if any):
  - You are pregnant.
  - You are responsible for a child under 16 or a young person.
  - You are aged 16/17.
  - You qualify for a disability premium as part of your Income Based Job Seeker's Allowance.
  - You are a carer.

How to claim

As soon as you hit a problem as above with your Job Seeker's Allowance, tell the Jobcentre. You will be interviewed and will have to make and sign a 'hardship statement'. This will cover details of your personal circumstances, savings, any money coming in, any debts and other benefits being received. If you are saying your hardship is linked to medical problems, you may have to give permission for the Jobcentre to contact your GP.

Amount box

You usually will be paid your entitlement for Income Based Job Seeker's Allowance (see *Amount box* for this benefit) minus 40% of what the Personal Allowance would have been for a single person of your age (even if you're claiming as a couple). If you, or your partner, are pregnant or seriously ill, the amount will be 20%.

You will normally be expected to make a 'hardship declaration' each time you sign on at the Jobcentre to confirm you are still in hardship.

Payment

If you fit into one of the categories above you will be paid from the date your Job Seeker's Allowance is stopped, otherwise you will be paid after 15 days of the suspension. You will be paid as long as you meet the qualifying conditions and you continue to sign the hardship declaration, so long as the Jobcentre accept you remain in hardship.

Health Service charges - claiming exemptions

There are fixed charges for some NHS items and services, such as prescriptions, dental treatment, sight tests, glasses, wigs and fabric supports. You will not have to pay these charges if you receive certain benefits. (See also *Health Service charges - help under the Low Income Scheme* and *Health Service charges - concessions.*)

Qualification checklist

- You, or your partner, receive Income Support or Income Based Job Seeker's Allowance.
- You, or your partner, have claimed Working Families' Tax Credit and have received a certificate confirming that you are exempt from charges. Not everyone who gets this benefit will get a certificate. If you are getting the set maximum Working Families' Tax Credit you will qualify; you will also qualify if you are getting up to £72.20 less than the set maximum (see the chapter on this benefit).

How to claim

In order to avoid paying prescription charges, fill in the back of the prescription before handing it to the pharmacist. If you want to avoid paying other NHS charges, ask for a form from the dentist, optician or hospital.

You will need to provide evidence that you are on one of the above benefits or, in the case of Working Families' Tax Credit, the certificate mentioned above. There will be restrictions on getting a voucher to pay towards glasses or contact lenses (as for *Health Service Charges - help under the Low Income Scheme*).

> **Amount box**
>
> If any of the *Qualification checklist* criteria apply to you, you will not have to pay the charges.

If you do pay, you can apply to the Health Benefits Division (see *Useful addresses*) for a refund, but usually you have to claim within three months. For prescription charges, use form FP57 (EC57 in Scotland) and for other benefits, use form HC1. These are available from the local Pensions Agency or Jobcentre Plus, or from some post offices. You will have to enclose proof that you had to pay the charge.

Health Service charges - concessions

There are fixed charges for some NHS items and services, such as prescriptions, dental treatment, sight tests, glasses, wigs and fabric supports but you may not have to pay them. (See also *Health Service Charges - help under the Low Income Scheme* and *Health Service Charges - claiming exemptions.*)

Qualification checklist

You are exempt from <u>all</u> the charges if:

- You are a permanent resident in a residential care or nursing home and your place is being at least partly funded by the local council (e.g. Social Services Department).
- You are a war disablement pensioner and you need the NHS item or service because of your war disability.
- You are aged 16 or 17 and the local council is maintaining you financially after you have been in local council care on or after 1 October 2001.
- You are an asylum seeker, or a dependant of one, who is receiving support from the National Asylum Support Service or a local council.
- You are aged under 16 (under 18 for dental charges) unless you are in full-time education, then you are exempt until you are under 19.

If none of these apply to you, you are exempt from prescription charges if:

- You are aged 60 or over.
- In Wales only, you are exempt if you are under 25.
- You are pregnant, or have given birth in the last 12 months.

- You suffer from one or more of the following illnesses: continuing physical disability which prevents you leaving your home except with the help of another person; epilepsy requiring continuing anti-convulsive therapy; a permanent fistula, including a caecostomy, ileostomy, laryngostomy or colostomy, needing continuous surgical dressing or an appliance; diabetes mellitus (except where treatment is by diet alone), diabetes insipidus and other forms of hypopituitarism, myxoedema, hypoparathyroidism, forms of hypoadrenalism (including Addisons disease) for which specific substitution therapy is essential; myasthenia gravis.

And you are exempt from dental charges if:

- In Wales only, you are exempt if you are under 25 or 60 or more, but only for the checkup.
- You are pregnant, or have given birth in the last 12 months.

And you are exempt from charges for sight tests if:

- You are aged 60 or more.
- You are registered blind or partially sighted.
- You have been prescribed complex lenses.
- You suffer from diabetes or glaucoma.
- You are aged 40 or over and you are the parent, brother, sister or child of someone suffering from glaucoma.
- You are a patient of the Hospital Eye Service.

Amount box

If you receive any of the benefits above, you will not have to pay the NHS charges at all.

What about vouchers for glasses or contacts?

- You are a patient of the Hospital Eye Service needing frequent changes of glasses or contact lenses.
- You have been prescribed complex lenses.
- The same restrictions apply to you getting a discount voucher as for Low Income Scheme to meet NHS Charges, except that here you cannot get a voucher if you damage or lose your glasses or contact lenses due to illness (unless you need complex lenses).

And wigs and fabric supports?

- You are a hospital in-patient where the wig or fabric support is supplied.

How to claim

If you are exempt from prescription charges because of your age or because you are a student under 19, fill in the back of the prescription before handing it to the pharmacist. In order to avoid paying other NHS charges, ask for a form from the dentist, optician or hospital. You may need to provide evidence of your age. If you are pregnant or have given birth recently, you can obtain exemption by filling in form FW8 which you can get from your GP surgery, midwife or health visitor. If you have one of the illnesses listed, apply for an exemption certificate on form FP92A (EC92A in Scotland) from your GP surgery, hospital or pharmacist. Send the form to the Health Benefits Division (see *Useful addresses*). If you are exempt because you are a war pensioner, contact the Veterans Agency (see *Useful addresses*). If none of these apply to you, you will need to use the same form HC1 as for people claiming on grounds of low income (see *Health Service charges - help under the Low Income Scheme*).

How to claim if you have paid

If you do pay, you can apply to the Health Benefits Division for a refund, but usually you have to claim within three months. For prescription charges, use form FP57 (EC57 in Scotland); for other benefits, use form HC5. These are available from your social security office. You will have to enclose proof that you had to pay the charge.

Health Service charges - help under the Low Income Scheme

If you do not receive the right benefits to allow you to avoid paying NHS charges, do not despair. You may qualify for help under what is called 'the Low Income Scheme' (see also *Health Service charges - concessions*).

Qualification checklist

- You have less than £8,000 in capital (or £12,000 if you or your partner are aged 60 or over, or £18,500 if you live permanently in a residential or nursing home).

- Your income is lower than what are referred to as your 'requirements'. Your requirements are based on the 'applicable amounts' for Income Support and Income Based Job Seeker's Allowance, although the qualifying rules are a bit more generous. They also include your rent and Council Tax, if any, less any benefit you receive, and any mortgage outgoings (interest and capital payments, endowment policy premiums).
- If you live with a partner or spouse, his income and capital will be included in working out your requirements.

How to claim

You will need to claim on form HC1 available from the local social security office and send it to the Health Benefits Division (see *Useful addresses*).

If you do pay, you can apply to the Health Benefits Division for a refund, but usually you have to claim within three months. For prescription charges, use form FP57 (EC57 in Scotland); for other benefits, use form HC5. You can do this at the same time as you claim on the HC1 above. The forms are available from the same places as the HC1 and you can claim at the same time as you claim under this scheme. You will have to enclose proof that you had to pay the charge.

Payment

If you are entitled to benefit, you will receive a certificate - form HC2 for full help, or HC3 for partial help. Show the HC2 certificate before you have to pay any charges. If you have the HC3 certificate you can only use it to get partial help with the items in the Amount box.

For purchasing glasses and contact lenses, the certificates will enable the optician or Hospital Eye Service to let you have a money-off voucher, but only if you need glasses or contact lenses for the first time, or your new prescription differs from your old one, or your old glasses have worn

Amount box

If your income is greater than your 'requirements', you will not have to pay the NHS charges at all, but if your income is higher, you may qualify for partial help, but only with the following:

- Dental charges and charges for wigs and fabric supports over a certain limit. (You may need to get a quotation on the charges, then take advice on how much you would be allowed).
- Sight tests.
- A voucher to buy glasses or lenses.
- Fares to hospital.

out in the normal course of wearing. You may also be entitled if you are under 16 and you have lost or damaged your old glasses or contact lenses and the cost of repairing them is not covered by insurance or warranty. The same may apply if you lost or damaged them as a result of being ill.

Your certificate will normally be available for six months, or 12 months if you are aged 60 or over, or entitled to a Disability Premium (in relation to Housing Benefit or Council Tax Benefit), or living in residential or nursing care. However, if you are self-employed, your certificate may last 13 months, and if you are a full-time student it should last until the end of your course or the start of the next academic year. A few weeks before your certificate expires you will need to claim for a new one, again on form HC1.

If your financial circumstances improve, this will not affect your entitlement to use the certificate until it expires, but if your finances get worse and you only have a partial help certificate you could claim for a full one.

With regard to prescriptions, fill in the back of the prescription before handing it to the pharmacist. A refund will be paid by Giro cheque.

Note that your employer should pay for sight tests and glasses if you work on computers a lot. See *In brief.*

Home Insulation and Energy Efficiency Grants

Here's a way to save on fuel costs. The Home Energy Efficiency Scheme (HEES) allows you to claim a grant to help cover the costs of home insulation and improving the efficiency of your heating. The scheme is called HEES in Wales, Warm Front in England, and the Warm Deal in Scotland.

Organisations called scheme managers or area agencies are responsible for the scheme in different parts of the country. You can either apply for a grant for them to do the work, or a grant where you make your own arrangements to do the work.

Qualification checklist

- You must occupy the property for which the grant application is made as your only residence, or, if you have other residences, this must be your main one.
- If you are claiming for the work to be carried out by a scheme manager, you must either own or rent the property.

- If you are claiming a grant to do the work yourself, you must own the freehold of the property or own the leasehold and have 21 or more years to run on it.

- You or your partner must be receiving Child Benefit for at least one child under 16, or (in England only) you must be pregnant and receiving either Income Support, Income Based Job Seeker's Allowance, Housing Benefit, Council Tax Benefit, Working Families' Tax Credit or Disabled Person's Tax Credit.

- If you don't have children, you still qualify if you receive any of the following: Income Support, Housing Benefit, Council Tax Benefit (if it includes a disability premium), Attendance Allowance, Disability Living Allowance, Industrial Injuries Disablement Benefit (if it includes Constant Attendance Allowance), War Disablement Pension (if it includes Constant Attendance Allowance) or Mobility Allowance.

- If you receive none of these benefits in England and Wales, you can still apply for a grant to do work yourself if you are 60 or over and you receive Income Support, Housing Benefit, Council Tax Benefit (if it includes a disability premium), Attendance Allowance, Disability Living Allowance, Industrial Injuries Disablement Benefit (if it includes Constant Attendance Allowance), War Disablement Pension (if it includes Constant Attendance Allowance or Mobility Allowance).

Amount box

The maximum grant is £1,500, or £700 if your major source of heating is mains gas, closed solid fuel room fires, solid fuel-fired central heating, oil-fired central heating or off-peak electricity.

The grant for you to do the work yourself is £250 in England, and the equivalent partial grant is £375 in Wales and £160 in Scotland.

How to claim

Contact Warm Front (in England), The Warm Deal (in Scotland) or the Home Energy Efficiency Service (in Wales) - see *Useful addresses*. They will connect you to your regional scheme manager and give you details of how to apply. When you apply, you will need to send in evidence of your eligibility for the benefits you are already receiving and say what work needs doing. This may be such work as cavity wall insulation, loft tank and pipe insulation, draught proofing of windows and doors and hot water tank jackets. Also, you may need space and water heating improvements such as gas room heaters with thermostatic controls, electric storage heaters, immersion water heaters and timer controls for electric heaters.

If you are eligible, a surveyor will be appointed to establish what is needed in your home. After that, the scheme manager will choose from among the contractors on their approved list in your area and arrange for them to do the work for you. You will also be given advice on energy efficiency.

If you have applied for a grant to do the work yourself, you will be given approval to start if it is deemed appropriate. Do not start the work until they have given permission.

Home Repair Assistance

Even the smaller scale repairs, improvements and adaptations do not come cheap, so this is a way you can obtain help to meet the bills.

Qualification checklist

- You are 18 or over.
- You must be an owner-occupier or private tenant but you may still qualify if you are neither of these but you have the exclusive right to occupy the property for at least the next five years.
- Usually you must be living in the property and it is your only or main residence, although this will not necessarily be the case if you are applying to help another person who lives in the property, or intends to live in the property, to be cared for. Such a person will have to be aged 60 or over, or any age if he suffers ill-health or is disabled or infirm.
- You are legally responsible for getting the work done.
- You must be receiving Income Support, Housing Benefit, Council Tax Benefit, Working Families' Tax Credit or Disabled Person's Tax Credit.
- However, it won't matter if you do not receive these benefits, if you are 60 or over, or if you suffer ill-health or are disabled or infirm. It also will not matter if you are applying for a grant to benefit someone who falls into these categories.

- You also have not applied for a House Renovation Grant, Disabled Facilities Grant or any other local council housing grant.
- You may also qualify if you live in a mobile home or a houseboat.

Amount box

The value of what you actually receive is up to your local council, but the maximum is £5,000.

What can be claimed for?

Your council will have its own priorities, but these are the kinds of assistance that will be considered:

- Making it easier for you to get access to your home, and rooms within.
- Making your home safe for you and anyone living with you.
- Enabling you to have easily accessible and usable bathroom and kitchen facilities.
- Improving or replacing your heating system to meet your needs.
- Making it easier for you to use power supplies, for example, for lighting and heating.
- Making it easier for you to move around the house to care for a dependant such as a child.
- Your local council have the discretion to make other grants available, for example, for adaptations which make your life at home easier.

How to claim

Your local council housing department will have a claim form and details of their priorities for grants. If you can fit your claim into these priorities, you will have a better chance of success. Assistance will be in the form of a cash grant, materials or a combination of both.

Home Responsibilities Protection (HRP)

Qualifying for certain benefits depends on your National Insurance record in what is called your working life (see the chapters on *Bereavement Allowance*, *Widowed*

Parent's Allowance and *Retirement Pension: Category A* and *B*). HRP enables you to disregard certain years so they don't count towards your working life and this improves your chances of qualifying for the full amount of these benefits later on.

Qualification checklist

The following tax years can qualify you for HRP but only if you have not paid enough National Insurance contributions, for example, because you're not earning enough.

- A tax year where you receive Child Benefit for a child under 16 - this must be for every week of the year.
- A tax year where you receive Income Support as a carer looking after a disabled person (see *Income Support if you are a carer*). Again, every week must be covered. However, if you are also getting Invalid Care Allowance, you get National Insurance credits anyway so you won't need HRP.
- A tax year where you spend at least 35 hours a week looking after someone who is receiving either the middle rate or higher rate of Disability Living Allowance Care Component, Attendance Allowance or Constant Attendance Allowance (part of Industrial Injuries Disablement or War Disablement Pension). You have to be caring for at least 48 weeks in the year but again, if you get Invalid Care Allowance, you won't need HRP.

How to claim

In the first two situations, you do not need to claim. These tax years will automatically count as years of HRP and therefore will not be included in years that make up your working life. With couples, usually the Child Benefit is claimed in the woman's name. If you as the man want to qualify for the protection, you will need for her to agree with your partner to stop claiming it so you can claim it in your name instead.

If you qualify in the third situation above, or if you qualify for part of the year in one situation and part of the year in another, apply to the Inland Revenue on form CF411. You can get this from your local social security office. Do this within three years of the end of the tax year in question.

Home Security Grant

Depending on where you live, you may be able to apply for a grant to improve your security at home, for example, burglar alarms and door and window locks. You will need to claim under the Home Energy Efficiency Scheme (HEES) under a scheme called Warm Front, in England and the Home Energy Efficiency Service, in Wales.

Qualification checklist

See *Home Insulation and Energy Efficiency Grants* as the Qualification checklist is the same.

Amount box

In England, the maximum grant is £2,500; in Wales, it is £2,700.

How to claim

See the chapter on *Home Insulation and Energy Efficiency Grants* as the procedure and *Useful addresses* are the same.

House Renovation Grant

Grants are available to help you carry out improvements or repairs to your home.

Qualification checklist

- Usually you must have lived in the property as an owner-occupier or private tenant for at least three years.
- However, the local council have discretion to waive this restriction, and it doesn't apply anyway if you are applying for a grant for a conversion, work related to fire safety, or if the property has been designated as a renewal area by the council (this is an area that the council has decided has unsatisfactory housing and wants to see improvements made).
- If you are a leaseholder, you must have at least five years left to run on the lease.
- If you are a tenant, you can qualify only if you are liable to carry out repairs to the property - see your tenancy agreement or take advice.
- The property must have been built or converted at least ten years prior to the application.

- Your income is below a certain amount. A means test is used to decide how much you should contribute. The council may also assess other people jointly with you if they are also intending to live in the property when it is renovated and if they are entitled to apply for a grant (for example, a partner or someone else you are sharing with). The means test is similar to Housing Benefit but more generous in some respects, for example, an extra premium is included in the applicable amount which is used for Housing Benefit (see *Appendix: Income Support, Job Seeker's Allowance: Income Based - the basics*).

Amount box

Once your contribution is calculated, this amount is deducted from the total cost of the works and the balance will be the grant. For example, if your contribution is held to be £3,527 and the total cost of the works are £12,500; the grant will be £8,973.

- If you have capital less than £6,000 this is ignored, but for every £250 extra you will be deemed to have £1 additional income. For example, if you have capital of £9,000, your income on this is deemed to be £12 per week (£9,000 - £6,000 = £3,000/250 = 12).

- If you are a landlord, you can also apply for a grant if you own the property and you let it out or intend to let it out. Take advice.

What can be claimed for?

A renovation grant can be paid to do the following:

- Bring a property up to the legal standard of fitness for human habitation, for example, making it structurally stable and providing adequate lighting, heating and water supply.

- Bring a property up to a standard of reasonable repair, for example, roofing work, window frames and doors, gutters and water pipes, damp proofing and wiring.

- Improving thermal insulation and energy efficiency, such as loft or water tank insulation and draught proofing, energy efficient boilers. However, you can also apply under the Home Energy Efficiency Scheme - see *Home Insulation and Energy Efficiency Grants.*

- Provide heating facilities - see also *Central Heating System Grant.*
- Improving internal arrangements, such as altering a room's layout so that a bathroom doesn't have to be accessed via a bedroom, or making a staircase less steep.
- Providing fire safety arrangements such as a fire escape.
- Converting a house into more than one dwelling (for example, into flats).
- Improve amenities such as the bathroom.
- Improve energy.

How to claim

Obtain an application form from the housing department of your local council. You will need to supply the details of your circumstances for the means test, the property details, a list of works for which the grant is required (usually two builders' estimates) and details of other fees. If you are an owner-occupier, you will have to sign a declaration that you or a member of your family intend to live in the property as your only main residence for five years after the works are completed. If you are a tenant, both you and the landlord will have to sign a declaration that you are liable to carry out repairs. You are advised not to start work until you have had approval!

The council will decide whether the repairs would be suitable for the property and the property would be fit for human habitation when you have completed the works. If they approve the grant, they will set a time limit within which you must carry out the works (usually 12 months).

Payment

Usually the grant is paid directly to the contractor. If you feel the work has not been done satisfactorily, you can ask the council to defer payment and they may agree to pay you instead so you can pay the contractor once the problems have been resolved. If you cease to be entitled to the grant, for example, because you leave the property within five years or you fail to get the works done in time, you may be asked to repay the grant.

Housing Benefit

Are you a tenant? If you are having problems affording your rent, then consider Housing Benefit. This is a means-tested benefit, designed to meet housing costs, whether you rent a flat, a house or a room in a hostel or a bed and breakfast; whether you are a private tenant, council tenant, joint tenant, sub-tenant, boarder or flat sharer.

Qualification checklist

The following conditions must apply to you:

- You, or your partner, are legally liable to pay the rent, i.e. you could be sued if you failed to pay. Even if you are not legally liable, you could still qualify if someone else - say your partner or spouse, or another person - is liable but he has left and stopped paying and you are left having to pay the rent in order to carry on living there.
- You are claiming for rent for a home you normally live in (although if you've signed a tenancy agreement but not moved in yet, you may be able to receive benefit for up to four weeks before you move in, and in some cases, if you're temporarily away, you may still qualify).
- You must have capital of not more than £16,000, that is any lump sum or one-off payment, savings or property. If the value of this is over this amount, it may be worth taking advice because some capital can be ignored so you could still qualify.
- Your or your partner's income must be below a certain amount (see *Amount box*).
- Some of your income is ignored or partially ignored. For example, your pay is only counted after tax and National Insurance and 50 per cent of contributions towards a pension scheme have been taken off. Other work expenses such as the cost of running a car, telephone and postage, special clothing may also be taken off but take advice. Then a further £5 per week is ignored (£10 if you are a couple, £25 if you are a single parent, or £20 if you or your partner are a carer or disabled, and an extra £11.65 if you or your partner work 30+ hours a week and you are bringing up children). Disability Living Allowance or Attendance Allowance is ignored, as are some childcare expenses. Take advice.

- The rules on income from tenants or boarders, and interest on savings are the same as for Income Support (see *Appendix: Income Support, Job Seeker's Allowance: Income Based, Minimum Income Guarantee and Disability Income Guarantee - the basics*).

Amount box

If you are claiming Income Support or Income Based Job Seeker's Allowance, you will be allowed the maximum Housing Benefit. This will meet all your 'eligible rent' minus any deductions set out below that might apply to you.

Otherwise, the amount of Housing Benefit you'll actually get, up to the maximum, will be based on your applicable amount. This can be worked out by totalling up all the elements that might apply to you in the Amount box in the *Appendix: Income Support, Job Seeker's Allowance: Income Based, Minimum Income Guarantee and Disability Income Guarantee - the basics*. These elements make up what is called your 'applicable amount'.

If your income is less than, or equal to, your applicable amount, then you will get the maximum Housing Benefit. If, on the other hand, your income is greater than your applicable amount, the amount of Housing Benefit you will get (if any) will be the maximum Housing Benefit minus 65% of the difference between your income and the applicable amount.

So, for example, if your eligible rent is £64 per week and you have no non-dependants living in your home, your maximum Housing Benefit is also £64. If your applicable amount is £84.65 because you are claiming as a couple, and your income is £140 (after ignored income is taken off), you are left with a difference of £55.35. 65% of this difference is £35.98. The Housing Benefit you will receive is therefore the £64 maximum minus this £35.98, which comes to £28.02.

What may reduce your entitlement?

Your Housing Benefit may be less than in the Amount Box, because:

- The council will only allow you Housing Benefit on what is called your 'eligible rent'. This is not necessarily the actual rent you pay. For one thing, water or fuel charges will be excluded, although service charges may be allowed. Also, your actual rent may be restricted as the council may ask the local rent officer service to decide whether the rent you are paying is too high for the area you are living in, or you are paying rent for a home too large for your needs. As a result, they may restrict your rent to what they think you should be paying.

- Also, if you are a single person under the age of 25, they will usually restrict your rent to the level that a person will pay in your area for a single bedroom where kitchen and bathroom facilities are shared. This will apply regardless of how many rooms you actually rent.
- If you are jointly liable with one or more other people (not a spouse or partner), your benefit may only be considered for a share of the rent, for example, it may be divided by three if you are all joint tenants in a house.
- If you have other people (called non-dependants) living in your home, such as an adult son or daughter, or grandmother, a deduction will be made from your 'eligible rent' before your maximum Housing Benefit is arrived at. This amount will depend on their earnings.

New tenancy? Helping you to decide

What if you're looking for somewhere to live and you are not sure if you can afford the rent? You can ask the council for what is called a pre-tenancy determination to see how much of your rent could be met by benefit. You'll need to give details of the proposed rent and the type of accommodation, and ask the landlord to consent to an inspection.

How to claim

You claim from your local council. If you are also claiming Income Support or Income Based Job Seeker's Allowance, a special shortened claim form (NHB1) is included in your claim pack, available from the local social security office, Jobcentre or the DWP website at www.dwp.gov.uk. If you qualify for either of these benefits, the social security office will send this completed form to the council whose area you live in. The council may send you their own claim form if they need more information from you, but you will be paid from the date they received the NHB1. However, because the NHB1s have been known to get lost, it's a good idea to ask the council for the full claim form and claim directly, mentioning that you are also claiming Income Support or Income Based Job Seeker's Allowance.

If you are not claiming these other benefits, you'll need to claim directly on the full claim form anyway. Ask for the claim to be dated from the date you ask for it. The form will ask questions about your personal circumstances and those of your household, including details of income, savings, rent and any childcare or medical circumstances. You will need to supply evidence of all of these.

If you face a delay through no fault of your own, i.e. the council have all the information they need from you, you are still entitled to interim payments. If you've just started work so you are no longer entitled to Income Based Job Seeker's Allowance or Income Support, the council are supposed to give your claim priority so long as you claim - or at least advise them - within 14 days.

Payment

Be prepared for a delay in actually getting paid - many councils have a huge claims backlog.

Your landlord will automatically be paid directly if you are a council tenant, or in some cases, a housing association tenant. If you are a private tenant in arrears, the landlord may be able to get the council to pay part or all of your rent directly to him for a certain period of time. In all other cases, you can either have the benefit yourself or choose to have your landlord paid directly.

When the council notify you of their decision on your benefit, they will also advise you how long they will pay you for. This will depend on the council's policy, and your circumstances, but the maximum is 60 weeks. In order to make sure that your benefit is uninterrupted, you will need to send in a renewal claim in good time. You can do this up to 13 weeks before the end of the period. In fact, a claim made within four weeks of the end of a period may still be classed as a renewal claim, so you should still avoid a gap in payments, although there may well be a delay in the council processing your claim.

You must report to the council of any change of circumstances, such as changes in your (or your families') income, including benefits (never assume this happens automatically!), your rent or any family members, or others, moving in or out. This may result in your claim being reassessed and you getting more or less benefit, or no longer qualifying at all. Should you not do so, you will be asked to apply for benefit all over again (called a renewal claim). It is usually more convenient for you, with less disruption to payments, if you can get the council to reassess. They will definitely want you to do a renewal, for example, if you've stopped receiving Income Support or Income Based Job Seeker's Allowance, or you move house.

You may be able to continue to claim at the same rate if you start a job or increase your hours - see *Housing Benefit (Extended payments).*

Housing Benefit (Extended payments)

This benefit is to help you if you've just started a new job or increased your hours and as a result you will be coming off certain benefits. The reasoning behind it is that this is a time when you might suffer cash flow problems as you wait for your first pay packet.

Qualification checklist

- You must be starting a job (including self-employment) for 16 or more hours per week, or you are increasing your hours to that amount; or
- Your partner (if any) started a job of 24 hours or more per week, or increased his hours to that amount, or
- You qualify for Lone Parent Run On (see *Lone Parent Run On*).

Also,

- In either case, you must expect the job to last at least five weeks.
- You or your partner have been getting Income Support or Income Based Job Seeker's Allowance (or equivalent) for at least the last 26 weeks prior to the new job or extra hours.
- Any income you receive, or any capital you have, is ignored.

How to claim

You have to tell the Jobcentre and the council that you have increased your hours or taken a new job. This should automatically trigger payments to you. However, you will lose out if you do not tell them within four weeks.

Amount box

The weekly amount paid is usually the actual Housing Benefit you were getting in your last full week of being on Income Support or Income Based Job Seeker's Allowance.

Payment

Payment is for the first four weeks of full-time work, or, if you qualify for Lone Parent Run On, for the two weeks after that ends. If your rent changes during this period, or even if you move home, this has no effect (unless you become a council tenant then usually the Extended Housing Benefit becomes whatever your new rent is).

Of course, you can still claim ordinary Housing Benefit as a result of the new job or extra hours (see *Housing Benefit*). If you qualify for the same period as the Extended Housing Benefit, you'll receive whichever is the higher for those four weeks.

Housing costs - extra help

Are you receiving some Housing Benefit and/or Council Tax Benefit and are still finding yourself in financial difficulties? The Government has made extra cash available to local councils to pay to people in this situation at their discretion.

Qualification checklist

- You qualify for Housing Benefit or Council Tax Benefit.
- You can demonstrate that you need financial assistance on top of these benefits to help with housing costs and Council Tax.

There are a lot of costs that will not be even considered, such as costs not normally covered by Housing Benefit anyway (for example, service charges, water and sewerage charges, increases on your rent to cover arrears) so take advice.

Amount box

This is up to the council. For Council Tax, you will not be able to receive more than your weekly Council Tax liability. Payments towards housing costs can be no greater than those that you have to pay towards rent and other charges, so long as they are eligible to be covered by Housing Benefit in the first place.

Having said that, there are a lot of situations that may apply so it's certainly worth claiming. A good example might be where the rent officer has said your rent is too high and therefore you have a shortfall in your ordinary Housing Benefit.

How to claim

You claim from your local council - the same section that deals with Housing Benefit. Ask them for the claims procedure, and if possible, have a look at their policy on discretionary payments as this will help you make the best of your claim. You will have to inform the council of the grounds for your claim and any other information they require.

Payment

The period of payment is up to the council to decide. If the period expires, you may be able to ask them to consider a fresh claim. As for Housing Benefit, in some circumstances, your landlord may be paid directly.

Incapacity Benefit

This is the benefit you can claim for if you are suffering from ill-health, whether your illness is short-term or long-term. It is not means-tested but in most cases qualifying will depend on your record of National Insurance contributions.

Qualification checklist

All the following must apply to you:

- You are not entitled to Statutory Sick Pay.
- You are aged under 60 for a woman, or under 65 for a man. You may still qualify for short-term Incapacity Benefit only if you are 60-64 for a woman or 65-69 for a man but only if you became incapable of work because of ill-health when you were under these ages and you would have qualified for a Retirement Pension but you decided to defer claiming it.
- You are incapable of work, i.e. you satisfy what is called the 'own occupation test', and after you've been claiming for six months, you satisfy the 'personal capability assessment'. See how to claim below. Even if the above doesn't apply, you may still be treated as incapable of work in certain specific circumstances so take advice.
- You have been paid or credited with a certain minimum amount of National Insurance contributions in one of the last two complete tax years before the benefit year. (See *Amount box*.) A tax year runs from 6 April one year to 5 April the next year. A benefit year runs from the first Sunday in January so it is nearly the same as the calendar year. Therefore, if you are claiming in October 2003, the two tax years you will be looking at will be 2001/02 and 2002/03.

  If you do not meet the National Insurance qualification, there are certain exceptions:

Amount box

The amount of Incapacity Benefit depends on the length of time you have been receiving it and your age. You can also claim for an adult dependant but this depends on the level of his income.

Incapacity Benefit	*If you are under 60 (woman) or under 65 (man)*	*If you are over 60 (women) or 65 (men)*
Short-term (lower rate)		
Paid for the first 28 weeks so long as you continue to qualify (although you may receive Statutory Sick Pay instead).		
Basic rate	£53.50	£68.05
Spouse or adult dependant *(provided he is not earning more than these amounts - see below)*	£33.10	£40.80
Eldest eligible child	N/A	£9.65
Each other child	N/A	£11.35
Short-term (higher rate)		
Paid after you have been on the short-term lower rate (or Statutory Sick Pay) for 28 weeks. This rate lasts 24 weeks until you have qualified for a year.		
Basic rate	£63.25	£70.95
Spouse or adult dependant *(provided he is not earning more than these amounts - see below)*	£33.10	£40.80
For the eldest child	£9.65	£9.65
If you are not getting Child Benefit for this child, the amount is increased to £11.35. If you are getting the lone parent rate of Child Benefit for the same child, the amount will be reduced by £7.65.		
Each other child	£11.35	£11.35
Long-term		
Paid after a year of qualifying but see above exceptions.		
Basic rate	£70.95	N/A
Spouse or adult dependant *(provided he is not earning more than £53.95 - see below)*	£42.45	N/A
Eldest eligible child	£9.65	N/A
Each other child	£11.35	
Age addition *Paid if incapacity began before age 35*	£14.90	
Age addition *Paid if incapacity began between age 35 and 44*	£7.45	N/A

NB Whatever rate of benefit you qualify for, if you receive certain pension payments totalling more than £85 per week, your Incapacity Benefit is reduced by half of the amount your pension exceeds this £85. For example, if you have a pension of £100 per week, £7.50 will be deducted (£100 - £85 = £15, £15 divided into half = £7.50).

- Young people cannot be expected to have a good National Insurance record, so if you were aged 16 but under 20 when you first became incapable of work, and you've been in this state for at least 196 consecutive days, you may qualify. You must claim within three months. In some cases, you might be able to use this concession if you are older, for example, under 25 if you have been a full-time student, or in some cases older if you had claimed under this concession in the past. Note that you cannot qualify if you are under 19 and in full-time education.
- If you were widowed before 9 April 2001 and you were incapable of work before your spouse died or in some cases shortly after he died.

When you can skip stages

The idea is that you move in stages, from one rate of benefit to the other, the longer you qualify. However, there are a few exceptions. Any days you receive Statutory Sick Pay (SSP) count against the days you would have received the short-term lower rate, so for example, if you got SSP and still qualified after you left your job after six weeks, you would only have 22 weeks at this rate. If you had 28 weeks of SSP, you would skip this rate altogether.

If you receive the higher rate care component of Disability Living Allowance or are terminally ill, you can skip the short-term higher rate and go straight onto the long-term rate. If you claim and your last claim was up to eight weeks ago, you can carry on at the rate you left off on. So, for example, if six weeks ago you were on the long-term rate and you fell ill again, so long as you still qualify, you'll go straight on to that rate again. In some cases, the period can be longer than eight weeks so take advice.

Claiming for a spouse or adult dependant

You may be eligible to claim an extra amount for a spouse if he is not entitled to benefit in his own right. If he is 60 or over, you can claim even if you live apart so long as you pay towards his maintenance. If he is under 60, you can only claim if you live with him and you are bringing up a child together. However, for short-term lower and short-term higher rate Incapacity Benefit, you can only claim for him if his earnings are not more than the Adult Dependant rate (see *Amount box*). However, the earnings figure is taken nett of any tax, National Insurance, half of any contributions to a pension scheme, and certain other expenses such as childcare costs.

Alternatively, you may be able to claim for someone else if he is looking after a child for you - such as a partner, ex-spouse or another person. The earning rules are the same but if you employ him to look after your child, his wages and any other earnings he may have can be ignored if he does not live with you. If he does live with you, you can ignore the wages you pay him but you have to count any other earnings he may have.

Claiming for a child

You may also qualify for an increase for a child or children, normally if you are receiving Child Benefit for them (but not if you are on the short-term higher rate of Incapacity Benefit unless you are a woman of 60 or over or a man of 65 or over). You will also not qualify if you have a spouse or partner whose earnings are above a certain limit, but the limit depends on the number of children you have.

You will not qualify for an increase for your first or only child if your partner's earnings are £155 or more in the week before your claim, if his earnings are £175 or more you will not get the allowance for any second child either, and if his earnings are £195 or more you lose out on the increase for any third child and so on. For example, if your partner earns £193 per week and you have three children, his earnings are over the £155 limit so you won't get anything for the first child, the second child is also ruled out as it's over £175, but the third child is just eligible as his earnings are under £195!

Working while claiming

This benefit is for people who are considered to be incapable of work, but you are allowed to work under certain conditions without it affecting your entitlement. This is called 'permitted work'. You can do this for up to 26 weeks provided you do not earn more than £66 per week. Usually you will be expected not to work more than 16 hours a week. You can start another 26 weeks after an eight week break (in some cases, you may be able to skip the break) but after that, you will have to wait another year before you can start another 26 weeks. Within six weeks of starting this, you have to tell the Department for Work and Pensions (DWP) in writing.

As an alternative, you can work indefinitely so long as you don't earn more than £20 a week. (You can also do this whilst you are waiting to start another 26 weeks.) This can be as much as £66 per week if you are in supported work, or as part of a hospital treatment programme (i.e. work on a scheme where you are especially supervised because of your disabilities). In these cases, you need to let the DWP know in writing some time before you stop working.

How to claim

There are two routes for claiming depending on whether or not you are employed.

Employees initially should report their sickness to their employer. If you are still sick after three days, the employer should pay you Statutory Sick Pay - if you qualify for it - as part of your wages or salary. If they think you do not qualify, they should give you form SSP1. This includes your claim form for Incapacity Benefit. The employer should also give you this form when your Statutory Sick Pay expires after 28 weeks, or earlier if you lose your job.

Otherwise, claim by sending form SC1 to the local social security office, again after three days of sickness. This form is known as a self-certificate. and is available from your local social security office, Jobcentres, doctors' surgeries, hospitals and the DWP website at www.dwp.gov.uk. If your doctor provides you with a medical certificate, send that with the form. If you haven't got one that's not a problem for the first seven days but after that, you will usually need one if you're still claiming. If there is any delay in waiting for a decision on your claim, you may be able to claim an interim payment.

In order to qualify in the first six months of sickness, usually you only need to satisfy what is called the 'own occupation test', i.e. you are not capable of working in what is regarded as your regular occupation. This will usually mean that you will have to provide medical certificates from your doctor (although for the first seven days a self-certification will do). In order to qualify for longer than six months, you will usually need to satisfy the 'personal capability assessment'. This will entail having to attend a medical examination which assesses your ability to carry out certain activities. This may not happen straight away so you will still qualify as long as you provide the medical certificates.

Whilst you are claiming, report any change in your circumstances to the social security office. If you are a long-term claimant, they may decide to reassess your claim at some stage.

You can be disqualified from receiving the benefit for up to six weeks if the local social security office think that you have contributed to your ill-health, for example, if you are claiming as the result of an accident whilst drunk, you ignore medical advice, or you refuse suitable treatment without good cause. The Benefits Enquiry Line (BEL) can give you further information - see *Useful addresses*.

Income Support if you are a carer

Do you care for someone who is ill or disabled? If you have little or no other money coming in each week, you might qualify for Income Support.

Qualification checklist

Firstly, see *Appendix: Income Support, Job Seeker's Allowance: Income Based, Minimum Income Guarantee and Disability Income Guarantee - the basics*, as you must meet all the conditions set out in the Qualification checklist in that chapter.

Secondly, one or other of the following situations should apply to you:

- You are aged 16-60.
- You receive Invalid Care Allowance, or the person you are caring for receives Attendance Allowance or the middle or higher rate care component of Disability Living Allowance.
- You can also qualify temporarily - for 26 weeks at most - if the person you are caring for has claimed Attendance Allowance or Disability Living Allowance and he is waiting to hear the result.

Amount box

In order to work out your entitlement see Appendix: *Income Support, Job Seeker's Allowance: Income Based, Minimum Income Guarantee and Disability Income Guarantee - the basics.*

Also, if you have a mortgage see *Mortgage and other loans - help with repayments.*

How to claim

For information on how to claim and how you are paid see *Income Support if you are pregnant or have children* as the procedure is the same. The Benefits Enquiry Line (see *Useful addresses*) offer further telephone help.

Income Support if you are a student

If you are a student, you may be entitled to Income Support to help with your daily living expenses.

Qualification checklist

Amount box

In order to work out your entitlement, see *Appendix: Income Support, Job Seeker's Allowance: Income Based, Minimum Income Guarantee and Disability Income Guarantee - the basics.*

Also, if you have a mortgage, see *Mortgage and other loans - help with repayments.*

Firstly, see *Appendix: Income Support, Job Seeker's Allowance: Income Based, Minimum Income Guarantee and Disability Income Guarantee - the basics*, as you must meet all the conditions set out in the Qualification checklist in that chapter.

Secondly, one of the following situations should apply to you:

If you are a full-time student aged 16-19 and you are in 'non advanced' education (i.e. anything up to and including A-level):

- You are so severely disabled that you are unlikely to get a job in the next 12 months.
- You are an orphan, and you have no-one who is acting as your parent.
- You would be in danger if you lived with your parents (or any person acting in their place). This could, for example, be a situation where you might be in physical danger or where the stress might cause you harm.
- Your relationship with your parents is so poor that you cannot live with them (this is usually referred to as estrangement).
- You live apart from your parents because they are unable to support you as they are chronically sick or disabled, or they are barred from entering the country as immigrants, or they are in prison.

If you are a full-time student in 'advanced' education (i.e. beyond A-level, such as degree or postgraduate level, HNDs):

- You are a single parent living with your child aged under 16 (a foster child will count); see *Income Support if you are pregnant or have children.*
- You are a pensioner (aged 60+ for a woman or 65+ if you are a man) - see *Minimum Income Guarantee.*
- You are a student from abroad who is temporarily without funds.

- You are disabled or ill and you qualify for the disability premium or severe disability premium or you have been too ill to work for the past 28 weeks - see *Income Support if you are disabled or ill.*

- You are deaf and qualify for a Disabled Student's Allowance.

If the above conditions do not apply to you, you may still qualify for Income Support for the summer holiday only, if the following are relevant to your situation:

- You would have been eligible for Income Support even if you weren't a student, say as a carer, widow/er or bringing up children (see the relevant chapters on these situations).

- Also, you have a partner who is also a full-time student, and you are looking after a child (or children) (i.e. one of you receives Child Benefit).

Claiming and getting paid

For information on how to claim and how you are paid, see *Income Support if you are pregnant or have children* as the procedure is the same. You will also need to supply evidence that you are studying from your school or college.

Income Support if you are a young person on a training course

If you are a young person on a training course, you may be eligible for Income Support if you have little or no other money coming in each week.

Qualification checklist

Firstly, see *Appendix: Income Support, Job Seeker's Allowance: Income Based, Minimum Income Guarantee and Disability Income Guarantee - the basics*, as you must meet all the conditions set out in the Qualification checklist in that chapter.

Amount box

In order to work out your entitlement, see *Appendix: Income Support, Job Seeker's Allowance: Income Based, Minimum Income Guarantee and Disability Income Guarantee - the basics.*

Also, if you have a mortgage, see *Mortgage and other loans - help with repayments.*

Secondly, one or other of the following situations should apply to you:

- You are not employed but on a training course being provided by the Learning and Skills Council for England, the National Council for Education and Training for Wales, or a local enterprise company in Scotland.
- You are between 18 and 24 years old.
- You can qualify if you are aged between 16 and 18 if you are on the lower rate of Training Allowance, or if you qualify for a disability premium (see *Income Support if you are disabled or ill.*)

Claiming and getting paid

For information on how to claim and how you are paid, see *Income Support if you are pregnant or have children* as the procedure is the same.

Income Support if you are disabled or ill

Are you not able to work because of illness or disability? If you have little or no other money coming in each week, you might qualify for Income Support.

Qualification checklist

Firstly, see *Appendix: Income Support, Job Seeker's Allowance: Income Based, Minimum Income Guarantee and Disability Income Guarantee - the basics* as you must meet all the conditions set out in the Qualification checklist in that chapter.

Secondly, all of the following situations must apply to you:

- You are aged between 16 and 60.
- You are entitled to Statutory Sick Pay.
- You are incapable of work. The procedure for deciding whether you are incapable is the same as for Incapacity Benefit.

Amount box

In order to work out your entitlement, see *Appendix: Income Support, Job Seeker's Allowance: Income Based, Minimum Income Guarantee and Disability Income Guarantee - the basics.*

Also, if you have a mortgage, see *Mortgage and other loans - help with repayments.*

- If the first 28 weeks have passed and you have not yet had the 'personal capability assessment' you will still qualify so long as you still receive medical certificates from your doctor.
- Even if the above doesn't apply, you may still qualify if you suffer an infectious disease, or you are severely mentally or physically disabled or you are blind.
- If you are not treated as incapable of work because you failed the 'own occupation test' or the 'personal capability assessment' above, but you are appealing against that decision, you can still qualify at least until you know the outcome of the appeal, so long as you keep sending in medical certificates. However, if you are appealing against the 'personal capability assessment', you may have 20 per cent knocked off your entitlement.

Claiming and getting paid

For information on how to claim and how you are paid, see *Income Support if you are pregnant or have children* as the procedure is the same. The Benefit Enquiry Line (see *Useful addresses*) offer telephone advice.

Income Support if you are pregnant or have children

You may qualify for Income Support if you're bringing up children and you have little or no other money coming in each week.

Qualification checklist

Firstly, see *Appendix: Income Support, Job Seeker's Allowance: Income Based, Minimum Income Guarantee and Disability Income Guarantee - the basics*, as you must meet all the conditions set out in the Qualification checklist in that chapter.

Secondly, one or other of the following situations should apply to you:

- You are a single parent bringing up a child under 16 on your own.
- You are bringing up a child alone because your partner is temporarily out of the country.

- You are looking after a child because the person who normally does it is ill or temporarily away.
- You are pregnant and you are expecting the baby within 11 weeks (you will qualify during the rest of your pregnancy if your doctor says you are incapable of work).
- You had a baby within the last seven weeks.
- You are looking after one of your children living with you, because he is temporarily ill. (The child could be of any age, up to 19, if you are getting Child Benefit for him.)

Amount box

In order to work out your entitlement, see *Appendix: Income Support, Job Seeker's Allowance: Income Based, Minimum Income Guarantee and Disability Income Guarantee - the basics.*

Also, if you have a mortgage, see *Mortgage and other loans - help with repayments.*

How to claim

Claim on form A1, or form B16 if you are self-employed. These are available from the local social security offices or from the website at www.dwp.gov.uk.

If you are reclaiming Income Support within 12 weeks of previously getting the benefit entitlement, and there's been no change in your circumstances since then, you may be able to complete a simpler and shorter 'Rapid Reclaim' form.

The claim form includes a section for claiming Housing Benefit and Council Tax Benefit. This section will be sent to the local authority so that they can assess whether you are entitled. If you think you are eligible, it is a good idea to claim these separately from the local council as well, to help reduce likely delays.

You'll need to supply ID and evidence of your circumstances when you apply. Your claim will probably be dealt with by post, although you may have to attend an interview or be visited at home. If you are a single parent and your youngest child is over five years three months, you will be interviewed to discuss what steps you can make to improve your job prospects (such as training and job hunting). You can claim money towards your fares if you are asked to attend the social security office. Single parents making new claims may be visited at home to discuss applying for Child Support (Child Maintenance).

Income Support if you are widowed

If you have been widowed, you may be eligible for Income Support if you have little or no other money coming in each week.

Qualification checklist

Firstly, see *Appendix: Income Support, Job Seeker's Allowance: Income Based, Minimum Income Guarantee and Disability Income Guarantee - the basics*, as you must meet all the conditions set out in the Qualification checklist in that chapter.

Secondly, one or other of the following situations should apply to you:

- You were aged 55-60 on 9 April 2001, and widowed on or after that date.
- You are single - not remarried or living with a partner.

> **Amount box**
>
> In order to work out your entitlement, see *Income Support, Income Based Job Seeker's Allowance, Minimum Income Guarantee* and *Disability Income Guarantee - the basics.*
>
> Also, if you have a mortgage, see *Mortgage and other loans - help with repayments.*

Claiming and getting paid

For information on how to claim and how you are paid, see *Income Support if you are pregnant or have children* as the procedure is the same.

Independent Living (1993) Fund (ILF)

If you are disabled or suffer ill-health, you can apply for cash payments towards payment for care to help you live independently at home, for example, by employing care assistants.

Qualification checklist

All payments are discretionary, but normally these rules are applied. You must meet the following criteria:

> **Amount box**
>
> Usually the maximum amount you can receive is £395 a week but in exceptional cases there may be more.

- You are severely disabled to the extent that you need extensive help with personal care or household duties to enable you to live independently in the community.
- You are aged 16 to 66 and receiving Disability Living Allowance (DLA) higher rate care component.
- You are receiving Income Support or Income Based Job Seeker's Allowance or have an income of about that level after a set amount is paid towards your care costs.
- You have less than £18,500 in savings.
- You are living alone or with people who are unable to fully meet your care needs.
- The local council Social Services Department supports your claim.
- If all these do not apply to you, you may still be able to claim if you are doing it on behalf of someone it does apply to, but they are not able to do it themselves or will not be able to manage the money themselves.

NB The Government have recently announced a similar scheme for older people receiving Attendance Allowance - take advice.

How to claim

Get in touch with your local council Social Services Department. Ask them for an assessment of your needs and say that you want to apply to the Independent Living Fund (ILF) 1993 Fund. Your application to the ILF (see *Useful addresses*) will be supported by the Social Services if the assessment shows that the care package you need will cost them at least £200 per week, so long as it will not cost the Social Services and the ILF fund together more than £665 per week. The next stage will be for an ILF visiting social worker to meet with you and a council social worker to jointly agree with you on the amount and type of care you need. The ILF social worker will produce a written report making recommendations to the ILF, and the ILF will decide whether to pay you, and how much per week so long as it is within the maximum. Before they arrange to pay you (usually directly into your bank account), the ILF will ask for details of your care assistants and how much you intend to pay each one.

You will have to pay a contribution towards the ILF grant. The exact amount will be worked out by the ILF depending on your income, although some of your income and any earnings you have will be ignored. If you are charged by the Social Services Department for care they are providing, this charge will be deducted from the amount ILF say you should contribute.

If your care needs increase, you must discuss this with your social worker. You can go back to the ILF to ask them to consider increasing the payments and they may try to get the Social Services Department to increase their contribution. If you have been receiving ILF funds for some time (at least more than six months approximately) increased payments may be agreed that could take you over the above combined £665 maximum.

Industrial Disablement Benefit

You may qualify for Industrial Disablement Benefit if you've become ill or disabled because of something that happened at work. Claiming this benefit does not imply that you are holding your employer responsible as you can qualify whether or not they were to blame. Also, you can remain entitled whether or not you are working.

Qualification checklist

All of the following must apply to you:

- You were a paid employee (not self-employed) at the time of the accident or illness. It usually does not matter if it is your first day in the job. (There are some exceptions such as occupational deafness where you have to have been working in a particular occupation for at least 10 years.)
- You have had a Declaration from the social security office that you had the accident or became ill in the course of your paid employment, and your job caused it to occur.
- If you are claiming because of an illness, the illness is listed as a 'prescribed industrial disease'. This is a list of diseases which are known to have links to particular occupations (these are called prescribed occupations). Take advice to see if your illness is on the list.

- It is not enough to have this disease. You also have to prove that you worked in one or more of the jobs in the prescribed occupation relevant to the disease, and that this particular job caused the disease.
- As a result, you are assessed to be at least 14 per cent disabled. However, there are certain exceptions to this. For example, if you contracted pneumoconiosis or certain respiratory diseases, you can qualify even if your assessment is just 1 per cent.
- 15 weeks have elapsed since the date of the accident or since you became ill (although if you have the disease mesothelioma this waiting period does not apply).
- In addition, you may qualify for one or more of the following benefits on top of your Industrial Disablement Benefit:
    - Constant Attendance Allowance: Applicable if you are receiving Industrial Disablement Benefit for 100 per cent disablement assessment and are so disabled that you are dependent on constant care and attention (and likely to remain so for a prolonged period). The higher rate (see *Amount box*) applies if you are entirely (or almost entirely) dependent on care full-time, and the lower rates, if you are to a great extent dependent either full- or part-time.
    - Exceptionally Severe Disablement Allowance: Applicable if you are entitled to Constant Attendance Allowance at more than the basic rate.
    - Reduced Earnings Allowance (REA): Applicable if your accident or illness occurred before 1 October 1990 and you are still suffering from the effects. You only have to have a disablement assessment of 1 per cent or more.
    - Retirement Allowance: Paid instead of REA if you are getting REA when you reach pension age (60 for women, 65 for men).

What if you have an accident whilst travelling?

Ordinary travelling to and from work does not usually count, but there are exceptions. If your employer especially arranges the transport, or it is operated by them or on their behalf, then you may qualify. You may also qualify if you are travelling on the employer's business say to a meeting, or if you have no place of work as such (for example, a truck driver). There have been different interpretations of this area so it is best to take advice, particularly if you disagree with a DWP decision.

Amount box

You can read from this chart how much you will get depending on your disability assessment, but if your percentage isn't on the chart, you may have to round it up or down. If you are assessed at between 14% and 19%, this is treated as 20%. If you are more than 20%, percentages over 20% are rounded to the nearest multiple of 10%, so, for example, if you are assessed at 21-24% it is rounded down to 20%, but if you are 25-29% it is rounded up to 30%.

INDUSTRIAL DISABLEMENT BENEFIT

Assessed disablement	*If you are under 18* £	*If you are 18 or over, or if you are under 18 but with dependants* £
100%	70.35	114.80
90%	63.32	103.32
80%	56.28	91.84
70%	49.25	80.36
60%	42.21	68.88
50%	35.18	57.40
40%	28.14	45.92
30%	21.11	34.44
11-20%	14.07	22.96
1-10% - only paid in the case of certain diseases or Reduced Earnings Allowance - take advice	7.04	11.48

INCREASES YOU MAY QUALIFY FOR ON TOP OF INDUSTRIAL DISABLEMENT BENEFIT

Constant Attendance Allowance	Higher rate	92.00
	Lower rates	
	Full-time care and attention	46.00
	Part-time care and attention	23.00 (or whatever is held to be reasonable in the circumstances
	Extent of care and attention greater due to exceptional disablement	Up to 69.00
Exceptionally Severe Disablement Allowance		46.00

Reduced Earnings Allowance (REA)	Broadly speaking the amount you receive will be the difference between your current earnings (if any) and the earnings you would have received had the accident or illness not occurred. The amount should increase along with increases in wages in the job, and promotion you may have attained. The maximum payment is £45.92 per week. If you are receiving industrial disablement and REA, the maximum is £160.72 per week.
Retirement Allowance	£11.48 per week, or 25% of the REA you were getting, whatever is the lower.

How to apply for a Declaration

Before you can claim for the accident, you must have a Declaration from the social security office that you have had an industrial accident. In order to apply for a Declaration, you need form B195 available from the Benefits Enquiry Line (BEL) or your local social security office, or from the website at www.dwp.gov.uk. It is wise to apply even if you don't intend claiming at present due to the fact, for example, that you do not feel any ill effects. If you leave it too late it may be difficult for the office to decide in your favour as the employer may have forgotten that the incident or the records may have been destroyed. The social security office will contact your employer, and will only send you a Declaration if they are satisfied that at the time of your accident you were a paid employee, and that the accident was in some way caused by your job during the course of this employment.

NB If you have an accident at work, remember to record it in the accident book, as this evidence may be crucial later.

How to claim

The above sources will be able to provide you with the claim form you need - there are different ones depending on your illness or the type of accident you had. If you had an accident/disease some years ago, you may still be able to claim if you are still suffering from the effects. Even if you have already claimed and have been turned down, it may be worth reapplying if you feel your disability has got worse. Send your claim form to your local social security office. You may have to have a medical examination.

Payment

It is possible you may be given a provisional disability assessment for a fixed time period because the medical examiner considered that your condition had not yet settled down, and might get worse or better. Before the end of the time period, you will be invited for a further medical so that a final assessment can be made. Your assessment should include the psychological effects of the accident or illness as these may affect your disability.

Depending on the nature of your disability, your final assessment may be for a limited period or for life. If, in your case, it is a limited period - if you are still disabled - you will need to apply for a renewal of benefit. In order to avoid a gap in payments, you should do this approximately three months before the fixed period expires. If you do not renew your claim because you feel better, then later you get worse again, you can reapply. You will not have to wait for another three months.

At any time if your health deteriorates and you feel that you condition has deteriorated, you can apply to the local social security office for what is called a supercession, i.e. to have your case reviewed. This may result in you receiving increased benefit. For further advice, contact the Benefits Enquiry Line (see *Useful addresses*).

Invalid Care Allowance (ICA) (to be renamed Carer's Allowance from April 2003)

If you are caring for a person with a disability or in poor health, you may qualify for this benefit. It is not means-tested.

Qualification checklist

The following must apply to you:

- You are aged over 16 (as from 28 October 2002 you can claim if you are over 65).
- You spend at least 35 hours a week caring for the person. This is an actual figure not an average, and the hours must be devoted to caring for the one person. However, if he does not live with you all the time, these 35 hours can include time spent preparing for his stay or tidying up after he's gone.

- The person you are caring for must be claiming one of these benefits: either the higher or middle rate of Disability Living Allowance Care Component, Attendance Allowance, constant Attendance Allowance in respect of industrial or war disablement.

- You are not in full-time education.

- You are not earning more than a certain amount per week (see *Amount box*) but this is nett of tax, National Insurance, 50 per cent of contributions to a pension scheme and certain other expenses such as childcare costs. However, your earnings are ignored if you work whilst the person you are caring for is in hospital, or you are having your break from caring (see below).

- If you share the caring with another person, only one of you can receive the benefit.

- If you care for more than one person, you cannot claim extra benefit.

Amount box

ICA is paid at a standard rate with increases for dependants. National Insurance contributions are not deducted but the benefit is taxable.

	Weekly rate
Basic allowance	£42.45
Increase for spouse or person looking after children	£25.35
Increase for first child	£9.65
Increase for each additional child	£11.35
Earnings limit for you	£72.00

Claiming for dependants

You may be eligible to claim an extra amount for a spouse if you are normally living together but this is not usually the case if you are a woman entitled to a Retirement Pension. Also, you cannot claim if your spouse is receiving certain benefits in his own right. You can only claim for him if his earnings in the previous week are not more than the Adult Dependant rate (see *Amount box*).

Alternatively, you may be able to claim for someone else if he is looking after a child for you, or for your children. The rules here are the same as for Incapacity Benefit.

How to claim

In order to claim you need form DS700 available from your local social security office, or from the ICA Unit (see *Useful addresses*), or local advice services, or from the Department for Work and Pensions (www.dwp.gov.uk). The claim should be sent to the ICA Unit as soon as the person being cared for has applied for Attendance Allowance, constant Attendance Allowance or Disability Living Allowance.

In any six-month period you are entitled to take breaks of up to four weeks and still retain your ICA.

Job Seeker's Allowance: Contribution Based

This benefit may help you if you've just lost your job.

Qualification checklist

The following must apply to you:

- You have been paid or credited with a certain minimum amount of National Insurance contributions in one of the last two complete tax years before the benefit year (see *Amount box*). A tax year runs from 6 April one year to 5 April the next year. A benefit year runs from the first Sunday in January so it is nearly the same as the calendar year. Therefore, if you are claiming in October 2003, for example, the two tax years you will be looking at will be 2001/02 and 2002/03.
- A certain minimum amount of the above contributions (see *Amount box*) must have been actually paid rather than just credited.
- You must be capable of working, i.e. you are not too ill to work. See the chapters on claiming *Incapacity Benefit* and *Income Support if you are sick or disabled.*

Amount box

Aged under 18	£32.50
Aged under 25	£42.70
Aged 25 and over	£53.95

If you receive occupational or personal pension payments over £50 a week, your Job Seeker's Allowance will be reduced by the excess. Therefore, if you get £60 per week, £10 will be knocked off your Job Seeker's Allowance entitlement.

- You will not qualify if you are in paid employment for 16 hours or more each week. However, there are certain exceptions, for example, if you or your partner are foster parents or if you are disabled and your earnings are 75 per cent or less than the normal pay for the job you are doing. Take advice.
- Even if you are working less, you still will not qualify if you earn more than a certain amount. This is the amount of the benefit (see *Amount box*) plus £4.99 (or £19.99 if you are a single parent or 60 or over or disabled).
- You are under pensionable age (60 for women and 65 for men).
- You fulfil what are referred to as the 'labour market conditions', which means the following:
    1. You are available for work, i.e. able to take up employment immediately in most cases. (You may be able to restrict your availability if you have a medical condition or disability.)
    2. You are actively seeking work, i.e. able to prove that you are seeking and applying for jobs. As a result, you will need to keep records and evidence, and attend the Jobcentre regularly.
    3. You hold a job seeker's agreement. This is an agreed plan of action with the Jobcentre on the steps you will be taking to find work.
- If you are a full-time student, you will only qualify in limited circumstances. There are also some restrictions on part-time students so take advice.

How to claim

In order to claim Job Seeker's Allowance, visit your local Jobcentre. You will be asked to fill in a claim form and provide supporting information. The claim form also enables you to apply for Income Based Job Seeker's Allowance (you can skip this bit if you know you don't qualify) but if in doubt apply! You will also need to fill in a form stating the steps you intend to take to find work, what kind of work, pay levels, etc, and then you will have to attend a 'new job seeker's interview'. If you are 16 or 17, you will have to register for work and training at your local Careers Service or Connexions. You can claim by post if the Jobcentre is so far away you would have to be away from home for eight or more hours and a Jobcentre officer will visit you at home.

If you are reclaiming within 12 weeks of your previous entitlement and there has been no change in your circumstances since you last claimed, you can complete a simpler and shorter 'Rapid Reclaim' form, also obtainable from the Jobcentre.

You will have to 'sign on' at the Jobcentre regularly - in most cases every fortnight - to show that you continue to meet the labour market conditions. If you live a long way from the Jobcentre, you may be able to do this by post. You will also be asked to attend advisory interviews from time to time, when suggestions will be made about steps you can take to find work. Your travel expenses will be paid for, but not for the routine 'signing on'. If you don't go along with the suggestions, the Jobcentre may eventually direct you to take certain action to step up your search. If you still do not cooperate, they may suspend your benefit or even stop it altogether. If this happens to you, see *Hardship payments if you are unemployed.*

You may be disqualified from receiving Job Seeker's Allowance for up to six months anyway if the Jobcentre decide you left your previous job of your own free will or you were dismissed through your own fault. However, in many cases you may be able to avoid this penalty (for example, voluntary redundancy or being dismissed because you can't do the job) so take advice.

You are paid for a maximum of six months.

Job Seeker's Allowance: Income Based

If you are unemployed with little or no income, you may qualify for this in addition to Contribution Based Job Seeker's Allowance. This is a means-tested benefit, and can include some help with mortgage costs.

Qualification checklist

- To begin with, most of the conditions for Contribution Based Job Seeker's Allowance must apply to you, i.e. you must be capable of work, working less than 16 hours, under pensionable age (60 for women and 65 for men) and fulfil the labour market conditions.
- In some cases, if you are claiming as a couple, your partner must make a joint claim with you. This would be if at least one of you was born after 19 March 1976, is 18 or over, and neither of you are responsible for looking after children. What if your partner fails to claim? The qualification for Job Seeker's Allowance will still

depend on your partner's situation: you may be disqualified altogether; you could just get the rate for a single person (see *Amount box*) or you may still qualify in full.

- You also need to meet the same conditions as for Income Support - see *Appendix: Income Support, Job Seeker's Allowance: Income Based - the basics.*
- If you are a full-time student, you can claim if you are claiming as a couple and you are both full-time students and either or both of you are responsible for a child. However, you can still only claim in the summer holiday and you have to fulfil the rules above.
- Otherwise, as a full-time student you can only qualify if you are on a Jobcentre approved employment related course, or have taken approved time out of your course because of illness or a caring responsibility and now you are waiting to return to your course.

Amount box

Your entitlement is worked out in the same way as Income Support - see *Appendix: Income Support, Job Seeker's Allowance: Income Based - the basics*, and, if you have a mortgage, see also *Mortgage and other loans - help with repayments.*

How to claim

The procedure for claiming is the same as for Contribution Based Job Seeker's Allowance, except you will have to provide additional evidence of your circumstances as this is a means-tested benefit. In some cases, you and your partner will have to make a joint claim (see the *Qualification checklist* above) but otherwise you can choose between yourselves who should be the claimant. The benefit will be paid so long as you continue to qualify.

Letting out rooms: tax relief

Do you receive any income from rent? This may be because you have a lodger at home, or perhaps you let out a holiday home or rent a house out to tenants. The income you receive is taxable, but you can claim tax relief on certain expenses you incur. This will reduce your tax burden. For more information on tax reliefs and how to claim them, see *Appendix: Tax allowances and tax reliefs and your Tax Return - some general points.*

Qualification checklist

- You have to be receiving rent or other income from land or property in the UK or abroad.
- You cannot claim under this scheme and also claim relief under the Rent a Room Scheme for a lodger living in your home (see *The Rent a Room Scheme - tax relief if you have a lodger at home*).
- If you are renting out a furnished holiday home, it must be available for letting to the general public on a commercial basis (that is you are aiming to make a profit!) for at least 140 days in the year. Also, you must actually be letting it out for at least 70 of those days. However, there are some days that won't count towards the 70 - this would be if you let to the same person for more than 31 days in a row, in any seven-month period!

Expenses for which you can claim tax relief

In order to claim first of all, you have to work out the expenses you have incurred over the previous tax year. Only certain expenses qualify. These include:

- Gas and electricity charges where the tenant is not liable.
- Insurance premiums for buildings and contents where the tenant is not being asked to pay them.
- Maintenance, repair and redecoration costs (but not the cost of improvements).
- Water charges so long as you have to pay them, not the tenant.
- Any rent you yourself have to pay (if you don't own the property you are letting).
- In some cases, mortgage interest on the property you are letting but not if it's your main or only home - take advice.
- Management costs, including agent's letting fees and the cost of advertising for tenants.
- Your council tax liability on the let property.
- Extra services you provide the tenant where the tenant isn't charged.

- If you are letting part of the home you live in you can only claim expenses for the proportion let out. For example, if a third of the home is let, you can claim a third of the above expenses for the whole home.

- Capital expenses such as what you spend on fixtures and fittings.

How to claim

You claim the relief when you declare your profit from letting in your Tax Return. So if the income you received in the year was £2,500 and your expenses amounted to £1,000, you can declare profits of £1,500 (£2,500 - £1,000). You won't actually need to set out your expenses in the Tax Return if your total letting income is less than £15,000 over the year, but it's best to keep your own record in case the Inland Revenue decide to check up on you. If your income is more than this limit, there is a space in the Tax Return where you have to list the expenses.

Put all the details in the Land and Property supplementary pages of the Tax Return (or the Foreign supplementary pages if your property is abroad). However, if you provide extra services, for example, you have lodgers at home and you provide meals and clean their rooms, this may be classed as a business so you'll have to declare in the self-employed supplementary pages (see *Self-employment expenses: tax relief*).

If you have a lodger at home, you may be better off claiming tax relief under the Rent a Room Scheme. See *The Rent a Room Scheme - tax relief if you have a lodger at home.*

Lone Parent Run On

This benefit may help you ease cash flow problems if you are a single parent taking up a job or increasing hours and thus coming off certain benefits.

Qualification checklist

- You must be starting a job for 16 or more hours per week, or if you are increasing your hours to that amount.

Also,

- You must expect the job to last at least five weeks.

- You have been getting Income Support or Income Based Job Seeker's Allowance for at least the last 26 weeks prior to the new job or extra hours.

- You have been a single parent throughout this time.

- Any income you receive, or any capital you have, is ignored.

Amount box

The weekly amount paid is the same as the Income Support or Income Based Job Seeker's Allowance you have been getting immediately prior to starting the new job or extra hours.

How to claim

You have to tell the Jobcentre that you have increased your hours or taken a new job and this should automatically trigger payments to you.

Payment

Payment is for the first two weeks of full-time work. You then qualify for Mortgage Interest Run On if you have a mortgage. You may also qualify for Extended Council Tax Benefit, and, if you pay rent, for Extended Housing Benefit.

Maintenance payments: tax relief

You may qualify for tax relief on maintenance you pay to your former (or separated) wife or husband, meaning you will have less tax to pay. For more information on tax reliefs and how to claim them, see *Appendix: Tax allowances and tax reliefs and your Tax Return - some general points.*

Qualification checklist

- Only payments made under a legally binding agreement count. This may be a court order, a written agreement or a Child Support agency assessment. Payments you make voluntarily will not count.

- If you are directed to pay the maintenance to the social security office this will qualify you for tax relief.

- However, you only qualify to claim tax relief if you, or your former (or separated) spouse, were aged 65 or over on 5 April 2000. If you want to claim for tax years before that (you can go back six years), no age limit applies.

- You cannot get tax relief if your spouse remarries even if you are paying maintenance for your children.

How to claim

You can go back six years if you haven't been claiming. Claim the relief by declaring in the correct sections on your Tax Return the amount of your contributions in the previous tax year. Give details of the relevant court order or agreement, and dates, if you are claiming for previous years.

> **Amount box**
>
> You will get relief at the tax rate on a maximum amount of payments. This may change each year. For claims for 2001/02, the tax rate is 10% and the limit is £2,070. Therefore, if you are claiming for this year, the most you can claim is 10% of the maximum which works out at £207 (2,070 x 10%).

Married Couple's Allowance - to reduce your Income Tax

You may qualify for this tax allowance but you must be married. You don't actually receive it but it reduces your tax bill. For further information see *Appendix: Tax allowances and tax reliefs and your Tax Return - some general points.*

Qualification checklist

You qualify if, during the previous tax year (that is the 12 months ending 5 April), the following categories applied to you:

- You were married and living together for at least part of the year. Even if you lived apart, you can still qualify if neither of you intended the separation to be permanent.
- Either you or your spouse (or both) are born before 6 April 1935.
- You cannot claim Children's Tax Credit if you claim this allowance, so take advice to see which of the two allowances you'd be better off receiving.

Making the most of the allowance

The allowance is initially given to the husband in the year of the marriage but the wife can ask to have half the basic amount of the allowance due transferred to her. She can have the whole basic amount transferred to her, but the husband will have

Amount box - tax year ending 5 April 2003

The Married Couples Allowance has two elements: a basic amount of £2,110 and an additional age related amount. These add up to the following amounts:

	Maximum allowance	*Maximum Tax Saving (as the allowance gives a 10% reduction in your tax bill)*
If the older one of you reached age 67 or older in the tax year	£5,365	£536.50
If the older one of you reached age 75 or older in the tax year	£5,435	£543.50

If you got married during the year, you'll get one twelfth of the allowance for each month or part month you are married in the year. If you permanently split up during the year, you will be able to keep all the allowance until the end of the year.

However, the actual amount of your allowance may be affected by the husband's income. If he was aged 67 to 74 and his income was £20,870 in the tax year, the age related part of the allowance tapers off - the more his income is the less the allowance is, until it disappears to nothing. If he was 75 or over the same thing happens but the income limit is £21,410. The point at which the age related part is wiped out altogether depends on the ages of both spouses.

Age of husband during tax year	*Age of wife during tax year*	*Income level at which age related part of the Married Couple's Allowance disappears*
Under 65	67-74	£24,610
Under 65	75 +	£24,750
65 or 66	Under 67	£20,870
65 or 66	67-74	£27,580
65 or 66	75+	£27,720
67 -74	Under 75	£27,580
67 -74	75+	£27,720
75 +	Any age	£28,260

Note that the basic part of the allowance cannot be eroded in this way.

to agree jointly to this! The age related part of the allowance cannot be transferred from the husband. Normally, to transfer an allowance in this way, you have to request it before the start of the next tax year, and it takes effect from then (6 April). The exception to this is if you are married in the tax year itself, then you can request a transfer to take effect straight away.

You can also transfer all or part of the allowance to your spouse if you did not have enough income in the year to use up the allowance, and they have tax to pay. See Children's Tax Credit as the procedure is the same.

How to claim

In order to claim, you will have to submit a Tax Return - see *Appendix: Tax allowances and tax reliefs and your Tax Return - some general points* for guidance on how to do this.

Maternity Allowance

If you don't qualify for Statutory Maternity Pay (SMP), you may be eligible for Maternity Allowance if you are pregnant.

Qualification checklist

- You must be pregnant, expecting the baby within the next 11 weeks or you have just given birth.
- You must not be eligible for Statutory Maternity Pay from your employer.
- You must not be in paid employment during the 18-week Maternity Allowance period.
- You have worked full or part time for at least 26 weeks in the 66 weeks immediately before your expected week of childbirth. It doesn't matter if the 26 weeks are not consecutive or if you have worked for more than one employer.
- You have average earnings which are at least at the level of the Maternity Allowance threshold (see *Amount box*). In order to work out your average, you can select your best 13 weeks out of the 66 weeks mentioned above, but all the 13 must have been spent working in the same job or for the same employer.

Amount box

Standard rate *Paid if your average earnings are equal to or above £75 per week.*	£75
Variable rate *Paid if your earnings average £75 per week - so long as they are more than £30.*	90% of your earnings (up to a maximum of £75)
Addition for spouse or other adult dependant	£33.10

The Maternity Allowance threshold is £30.

The National Insurance low earnings limit is £75.

Claiming for a spouse or other adult dependant

You can claim an extra amount for your husband, even if you live apart, so long as you pay towards their maintenance. You will not qualify if his earnings in the week prior to your claim are no more than the amount of the addition itself (see *Amount box*), nor will you qualify if he is receiving certain benefits in his own right.

Alternatively, you could claim for someone who is looking after your child for you, such as a partner, ex-husband or children's nanny. The earning rules are the same but if you employ him to look after your child, his wages and any other earnings he may have can be ignored if he doesn't live with you. If he does live with you, you can ignore any wages you pay him but you have to include any other earnings he may have.

How to claim

Claim on form MA1, available from antenatal clinics or the local social security office, or the DWP website at www.dwp.gov.uk. The form should be returned to your local social security office together with your maternity certificate (MatB1) (obtainable from your GP or midwife) and, if you are employed, form SMP1 from your employer. Also, if you are claiming after the baby is born, you will need a birth certificate. Normally, the claim should be sent at least 21 days before you want the payment to start.

If there is a change in circumstances, for example, you are claiming for an adult dependant and his income increases, you should report this to the social security office as your benefit may be affected.

Payment

The allowance is paid for an 18-week period (called the Maternity Allowance period). You have a certain amount of choice on when to start receiving payments. The earliest time is the 11th week before the baby is due. However, if the baby is born before then, you can get paid straight away. The latest you can start is the first Sunday after the baby is born.

Maternity Grant (Sure Start Maternity Grant)

A Maternity Grant is a fixed amount made towards the cost of providing clothing and equipment for a baby.

Qualification checklist

- You or your partner are receiving Income Support, Income Based Job Seeker's Allowance, Working Families' Tax Credit or Disabled Person's Tax Credit at the time of the claim.
- If you are under 19 and are not able to claim any of these benefits in your own right, members of your family may be able to claim a grant for you if they themselves are getting one of these benefits.
- You are pregnant or have given birth to a child within the last three months or you have adopted a child less than one year-old or had a child by a surrogate mother.
- You can also qualify if you have a dependant child under 16 who is pregnant or has given birth to a baby within the last three months or you have had a stillborn child after you had been pregnant for at least 24 weeks.

How to claim

Claim on form SF100 (Sure Start). Your partner can claim on your behalf if you wish. The form is available from local social security offices, antenatal clinics or the DWP website at www.dwp.gov.uk. Part of the claim form asks you to obtain the signature of a health professional such as your doctor, midwife or health visitor. The claim can be made from the eleventh week before the baby is due and up to three months after the baby is born, or up to three months after the date of the adoption order or parental order. Send the claim form to your local social security office. You will need to provide a maternity certificate (MAT B1) or a note from your doctor or midwife stating the expected date of birth.

Amount box

There is a lump sum - £500 per child.

Milk - free of charge

You may qualify for free milk for a child.

Qualification checklist

One of the following has to apply:

- You are pregnant, and you, or your partner, receive Income Support or Income Based Job Seeker's Allowance.*
- Your child or children qualify if they are under the age of five and you, or your partner, receive Income Support or Income Based Job Seeker's Allowance.*
- Your child also qualifies if aged five to 16 and does not attend school because of a disability.*
- If your child goes to a Local Education Authority or a grant maintained school, and is under the age of five, milk may be provided by the school for the child. If this is the case, you will not have to pay if you receive Income Support or Income Based Job Seeker's Allowance. It is up to the school to decide who else will not be charged.

Amount box

If you qualify under the rules marked * above, you will receive one milk token a week. This can be exchanged for seven pints of milk (or eight half-litres). Alternatively, you can go to a child health clinic if your baby is under one and exchange a token for 900 grams of dried milk. In the other situations listed above, the milk provided is usually about one third of a pint each day whilst the child is in the care of a childminder, day care provider or school.

- In Wales, your child will automatically qualify for free milk at school if he is being taught for Key Stage 1.
- You look after a child or children for two or more hours in a day, and you are a registered childminder. (If your child is in day care, the day care provider, for example, a school nursery, should apply for every child in its care.)

How to claim

Claim from your local social security office. You will need to show your maternity certificate (MatB1) if you are pregnant. If you cannot find a supplier who is prepared to exchange milk tokens, you can go back to the social security office to ask to have them cashed in. If the child is at school, they will tell you how to register for your child to have free milk.

NB You can buy dried milk at a lower price whatever your income if you attend a maternity or child health clinic.

Minimum Income Guarantee

If you are 60 or over and you have little or no other money coming in each week, you may qualify for the Minimum Income Guarantee. This is the name given to Income Support for the 60+ age group. It is expected that this benefit will be replaced by the Pension Tax Credit from October 2003.

Qualification checklist

Firstly, see *Appendix: Income Support, Job Seeker's Allowance: Income Based, Minimum Income Guarantee and Disability Income Guarantee - the basics*, as you must meet all the conditions set out in the Qualification checklist in that chapter.

- However, the difference to the above-mentioned chapters is that you can possess as much as £12,000 in capital and still qualify.
- Also, you must be aged 60 or more.

Amount box

In order to work out your entitlement, see *Appendix: Income Support, Job Seeker's Allowance: Income Based, Minimum Income Guarantee* and *Disability Income Guarantee - the basics.*

Also, if you have a mortgage, see *Mortgage and other loans - help with repayments.*

How to claim

Claim on form MIG1, available from your local social security office or the Department for Work and Pensions at their website www.dwp.gov.uk/mig.

If you ring the Minimum Income Guarantee claim line (see *Useful addresses*), they can complete a claim form for you over the telephone. For further information on claiming and how you are paid, see *Income Support if you are pregnant or have children* as the procedures are the same.

Mortgage and other loans - help with repayments

As well as helping to meet your daily living expenses, Income Support or Income Based Job Seeker's Allowance can also include an amount to cover some of your mortgage.

Qualification checklist

You qualify if you are eligible for Income Support or Income Based Job Seeker's Allowance - see the chapter on these benefits which apply to your circumstances (for example, *Income Support if you are pregnant or looking after children*) and also *Income Support and Income Based Job Seeker's Allowance - general.*

How much of your mortgage or other loans will be covered?

- Not all loans count anyway. You can only include interest on a loan you have specifically taken to buy the home you live in, or to carry out certain repairs or improvements. It does not cover any other loans to pay off debts or to go on holiday. (A remortgage will count, but only that part which was to replace an original loan which would have qualified.) There are a few exceptions to this rule, for example, if you take out a further mortgage to buy out your ex-partner's share of the home, buying out sitting tenants or purchasing a freehold if you are currently leasehold.

- The rules on repairs or improvements that qualify are pretty specific, for example, repairs to your heating system, or provision of bathroom facilities, drainage so take advice. If part of your loan covers things that qualify, and the rest don't, then you'll get interest only on that part.

Amount box

The amount will depend on the weekly amount of your repayments, allowing for all the restrictions below.

- You will not be able to include any capital repayments, or any other payments, for example, endowment premiums. Usually you will have to be living in the home, although there are exceptions, for example, if you can't return home because of domestic violence or you're away from home because you are a full-time student elsewhere. Take advice.

- Usually you will only receive benefit for loans of up to £100,000, although the total of any loans you took out to adapt your home for a disabled person will not count towards the £100,000.

- Also the amount you receive may be restricted if the social security office decides you are living in a home too big for your family, or if it is thought that you could move to a less expensive area reasonably.

- A standard rate of interest is used to work out how much of your housing costs count, even if you have to pay more than this. The current standard rate is 5.34 per cent. However, if you pay less than 5 per cent, you won't be quids in. In this case, your housing costs are calculated from your actual interest payments.

  Here is an example. You pay £300 per month in mortgage interest, and this includes an extra amount you borrowed to replace windows. This amount is £27 per month in interest so the amount that counts will be £273. However, if you are paying a rate of 6.2 per cent, your housing costs will be worked out on the current standard rate at £267 per month. Therefore, in this case, the housing costs added onto your Income Support calculation will be £61.61 per week.

- If you have people living in your home such as an adult son or daughter, or grandmother, a certain amount may be deducted from your Income Support or Income Based Job Seeker's Allowance for housing costs. The amount will depend on their earnings.

- If you took out your mortgage before 2 October 1995, you will not be allowed any Income Support towards the repayments for the first 8 weeks. After that, you will be allowed only 50 per cent of the interest for 18 weeks. Thereafter you will get the full amount due to you. However, if you took out the mortgage on 2 October 1995 or later, you will have to wait 39 weeks before you get any cash help. This waiting rule may not apply to you in some cases, for example, if you or any partner are 60 or over, or if you are transferring from Income Support to Income Based Job Seeker's Allowance or vice versa.

How to claim

If you claim Income Support or Income Based Job Seeker's Allowance, Minimum Income Guarantee or Disability Income Guarantee and you wish to include in your claim a mortgage or loan, you will be given a form M112 to give to your lender. They will provide details of your mortgage or loan and return the form to the social security office. The office will then assess whether you qualify for help and how much you qualify for. Payment is usually made directly to your lender.

Mortgage Interest Run On

This curiously named benefit is designed to help you if you've just started a new job or increased your hours and as a result will be coming off certain benefits. The reasoning behind it is that this is a time when you might suffer cash flow problems as you wait for your first pay packet.

Qualification checklist

- You must be starting a job for 16 or more hours per week, or if you are increasing your hours to that amount; or
- Your partner (if any) started a job of 24 hours or more per week, or increased their hours to that amount.

Also,

- In either case, you must expect the job to last at least five weeks.
- You or your partner have been getting Income Support or Income Based Job Seeker's Allowance for at least the last 26 weeks prior to the new job or extra hours. At least on the day before your claim this must include help with housing costs, i.e. interest on your mortgage for a house purchase or other loans for repairs and improvements.

Amount box

The weekly amount paid is usually the same as you were getting for help with housing costs as part of your Income Support or Income Based Job Seeker's Allowance per week. See *Mortgage and other loans - help with repayments.*

- Any income you receive, or any capital you have, is ignored.

How to claim

You have to tell the Jobcentre that you have increased your hours or taken a new job. This should automatically trigger payments to you. However, you will lose out if you do not tell them within four weeks.

Payment

Payment is for the first four weeks of full-time work or, if you qualify for Lone Parent Run On, for the two weeks after that ends.

National Insurance credits

In some situations you can be credited with National Insurance contributions - this can help you to improve your National Insurance record. This may also help you qualify for certain benefits in the future, such as Contributory Job Seeker's Allowance, Incapacity Benefit, Bereavement Allowance, Widowed Parent's Allowance and Retirement Pensions: Category A and B .

Qualification checklist

In these situations you will be credited with contributions automatically:

- For each complete week you are receiving Incapacity Benefit, Income Support if you are ill or disabled, Maternity Allowance, Widowed Parent's Allowance and Bereavement Allowance, or Severe Disablement Allowance or Widowed Mother's Allowance (it is no longer possible to claim these last two benefits if you haven't already been receiving them), Invalid Care Allowance, Income Based or Contributory Job Seeker's Allowance and, in most circumstances, if you are receiving Working Families' Tax Credit or Disabled Person's Tax Credit.

- For any period you are signing on at the Jobcentre as unemployed as per the rules for Contributory or Income Based Job Seeker's Allowance, even though you are not receiving these benefits.

- If you are a man, in the tax year in which you reach 60, then for the next four years. If you are a woman, you cannot be credited here as you will have already reached state retirement age.

- In the tax year you reach 16 and for the following two years.

Here are the main situations where you normally have to apply for credits:

- For any period you are incapable of work, as per the rules for Incapacity Benefit, even though you are not receiving the above benefits.
- You are pregnant and are not entitled to Maternity Allowance or Statutory Maternity Pay from six weeks before the baby is due until two weeks after.
- For each week you are on an approved training course. The course must be full-time (or at least 15 hours a week if you are disabled) and technical or vocational in nature. You must be aged 18, or reach 18, during the tax year.
- For any weeks you were imprisoned for convictions or offences which were subsequently quashed by the courts.
- For any weeks or part weeks you were on jury service.

How to claim

Take advice from the National Insurance Contributions Office (part of the Inland Revenue) to see whether it will help you to claim credits as above. Different credits may help you qualify for different benefits. There is usually a time limit - this is the end of the year following the year you were entitled to the credit. Therefore, if you were entitled in 2001, you should claim by the end of 2002.

Parking concessions

Throughout the European Union, you can apply for the Blue Badge if you are disabled or you carry a disabled passenger. This gives you a number of parking concessions.

Qualification checklist

- You can apply at any age but for a child, he must be aged 2 or over.

One of the following must apply to you:

- You are receiving the higher rate mobility component of Disability Living Allowance or War Pensioner's Mobility Supplement (see *War Disablement Pension*).

- You are getting a car supplied under a government scheme or a grant towards the purchase of your car.
- You are registered blind.
- You drive regularly and have a severe disability in both arms so you can't turn a steering wheel by hand, even with a turning knob.
- You have a permanent disability which makes it difficult or impossible to walk.

What the Blue Badge allows you to do

You will be able to park without charge or time limit at on-street parking meters and Pay and Display bays. In streets where waiting is allowed for only limited periods, you will be able to park for longer.

However, you must keep to all other parking restrictions, for example, you cannot park in a bus lane or cycle lane whilst it is operating, or where loading or unloading is banned. The rules may be different to an extent in your town, and concessions vary from one European Union country to the other so take advice. In parts of central London, you mostly have to use designated disabled parking bays.

How to claim

You apply to your local council and you may be charged £2.

Pension contributions: tax relief

If you are contributing to a pension scheme, you can claim tax relief on the contributions, meaning you will have less tax to pay. For more information on tax reliefs and how to claim them, see *Appendix: Tax allowances and tax reliefs and your Tax Return - some general points*.

Qualification checklist

One of the following has to apply to you:

- You are contributing to a personal pension plan (this could be a stakeholder pension plan if it was taken out after April 2001) and you earn less than £30,000 a year.

- You pay into your employer's occupational pension scheme.
- You are topping up the occupational scheme with free standing additional voluntary contributions (FSAVC).
- You pay into a retirement annuity contract (these were replaced by personal pension plans in July 1988 but you may well still be contributing).

Amount box

For retirement annuity contracts you are claiming the full tax relief at whatever rate you pay tax - basic or higher. Therefore, if you paid £1,000 in contributions and you are a basic rate taxpayer, you will get £220 in tax relief (1000 x 22%). For other types of pension contributions, you will automatically have received the basic rate tax relief on these contributions but if you pay tax at the higher rate you will be entitled to the difference between the higher rate and basic rate as extra tax relief. If, for example, you paid £1,000 in contributions and you are a higher rate taxpayer, you would have already received 22% (£220) automatically deducted as tax relief, but you can claim another £180 (40% of 1000 = 400; 400 - 220 =180).

There are maximum amounts of tax relief you can get on pension contributions depending on your age, income and circumstances. If you are over the maximum in the year you are applying, you may be able to take up unused tax relief in previous years by what is called 'carry back' or defer a claim till a future year ('carry forward'). Take advice.

How to claim

Check with the pension providers. With regard to pensions you take out through your employer (company pensions) and most pensions you take out yourself (personal pensions), tax is deducted automatically from the contributions at the basic rate. However, you may be contributing to an earlier type of pension which you took out yourself, called a retirement annuity contract. With this you may well need to claim your tax relief separately.

You can go back six years if you haven't been claiming and you will get relief at the tax rate you were paying in the year you made the contributions. Therefore, if you are claiming for the year 2001/02, for example, the basic tax rate was 22 per cent, so if you were paying at this rate you can claim 22 per cent as relief. The higher rate (if you earned more than £29,900) was 40 per cent so if you earned at this level you can claim relief at 40 per cent.

For all types of pension contributions claim the relief by declaring in the correct sections on your Tax Return the total amount of your contributions in the previous tax year. It is also possible to claim on this Tax Return the tax relief on the payments you have made in the current tax year. Of course, if you do so, you won't be able to claim the relief on these payments next time you fill out the tax return, but you will get the relief earlier. Even after you send in your Tax Return you can claim relief for payments in the current year; just ask the tax office for forms PP43 and PP120.

Pension Tax Credit (PTC)

The Government is planning to introduce this new benefit from October 2003. At the time of writing not all information on this benefit has been published, so if you have other queries, take advice.

Amount box

At the time of writing the amounts have not been published, but here is an outline of the main elements of PTC:

- **A guarantee credit - if you are aged 60 or over (this will replace Minimum Income Guarantee).**

  The maximum is expected to be £100 if you are single and £154 if you are claiming as a couple, with additional amounts for your housing costs, and if you are severely disabled (for example, receiving the higher rate care component of Disability Living Allowance or Attendance Allowance) or if you are a carer. (This will be similar to Minimum Income Guarantee.)

- **A savings credit - if you are 65 or over.**

  The amount you receive will be based on your income above a certain minimum amount, for example, from second pensions and savings. The minimum is likely to be the same as the amount of the basic Category A Retirement Pension up to a certain maximum. The rate paid will be at 60p for every £1. Therefore, if your income is £95.50 per week, for example, that's £20 above the current Category A pension, so your credit is likely to be £12 per week.

Qualification checklist

You qualify if the following applies to you:

- You are aged 60 or over.
- Your income is below a certain amount, although any capital you have (that is any lump sum or one-off payment, savings or property) will have no effect on the Tax Credit.
- If you work, the hours you do will not stop you qualifying.

How to claim

If you are getting Minimum Income Guarantee, you should receive a letter from the Pensions Agency inviting you to claim in time to be paid from 7 April 2003. Otherwise, see *Working Tax Credit*, as the procedure for claiming and getting paid is the same. The exceptions are that an income of around 10 per cent will be assumed on any capital over £6,000 (£10,000 if you are in a care home) and you can be paid for five years at a time. Also you have to claim from your local social security office, not the Inland Revenue. During this time, you will be able to declare any decreases in income so that your PTC can be increased accordingly.

Personal Allowance - to reduce your Income Tax bill

This is one benefit you don't have to claim. You don't actually receive it but it reduces your tax bill. This is an Income Tax allowance, administered by the Inland Revenue, available to everyone. For further information, see *Appendix: Tax allowances and tax reliefs and your Tax Return - some general points.*

Qualification checklist

- Available to all taxpayers and potential taxpayers from birth onwards.
- A couple are each entitled to a Personal Tax Allowance in the same way as single people.

Amount box - tax year ending 5 April 2003

	Maximum allowance
Aged 0 to 64	£4,615
Aged 65 to 74	£6,100
Aged 75 +	£6,370

If you are aged 65 to 74, the £6,100 starts to reduce if your income is above £17,900, at a rate of £1 for every £2 above this level, so that if your income is £20,870 or more, you only get the rate for 0 to 64 year-olds. The same thing happens if you are 75+ but the maximum income level is £21,410, after which you only get the 0 to 64 rate.

How do you claim?

Provided the Inland Revenue knows of your existence, you will be given this allowance without claiming it. They will know of you if you have submitted a Tax Return or if you are an employee, as your employer will have notified them of your details.

Redundancy Payments Scheme - if you are made redundant

If you have been made redundant from your job you may be entitled to a lump sum payment.

Qualification checklist

- In most cases you must have at least two years' continuous service with your employer.
- Service before you reach age 18 does not count.
- You do not qualify if you are made redundant at age 65 or over.
- In most cases you must have been been dismissed by your employer, and the reason for your dismissal must have been redundancy. This means that your dismissal must have been caused by your employer's need to reduce the

Amount Box

The amount you are entitled to will depend on the number of years you have been working for the employer or an associated employer, and the age you were from the date you began.

For each complete year of continuous service between the ages of:	*Entitlement*
18 and 21	Half a weeks gross pay (that is before tax and other deductions)
22 and 40	One weeks gross pay
41 and 65	One and a half weeks gross pay

However there are three big 'buts' which might reduce your entitlement:

- There is an upper limit on the amount of a week's pay that can be taken into account - this is currently £250 per week, so if your gross pay is £400 only £250 counts.
- Only a maximum of 20 years employment counts, so if you worked 26 years only the last 20 will count.
- And finally… once your full entitlement is worked out, if you are over 64, the total amount of the payment you receive will be reduced by one twelfth for each complete month you are over 64 - tapering off to nothing if you are 65 plus.

Having said all this, some employers will offer more generous redundancy payments, including what they may call severance payments. There may be more information in your written statement of employment particulars (your contract of employment) or staff handbook, or from your union, or your employer will issue a statement if redundancies are in the offing.

workforce - perhaps because the workplace is closing down, or because fewer employees are needed for work at a particular time.

- Two exceptions to this are if you are laid off (that is, you are asked not to work and you are paid no wages) or you are put on short time (your hours are reduced and you receive less than half a week's pay as a result). If either of these happens to you for four weeks in a row, or six out of 13 weeks, you may, if you wish, claim a redundancy payment. Take advice.

- If your employer says that redundancies will be needed and asks for volunteers, you will qualify for payment if you volunteer so long as your employer actually dismisses you.
- Normally for you to be redundant your job must have disappeared, but not in all cases. If you are made redundant because of a need to reduce the workforce, and one of the remaining employees moves into your job, you will still qualify for a redundancy payment so long as no vacancy exists in the area (that is the type of work and location) where you worked.
- You won't usually qualify if you are offered a new job with your employer, or an associated employer. However, the job must have been offered before your present contract ends, and you must be allowed to start within four weeks. If you feel your new job may be unsuitable, you can ask to work in this position on a four-week trial period (longer if retraining is required) and if it doesn't work out for you, you may still be able to claim a redundancy payment. Take advice.
- Also you won't qualify if you are offered a job by an employer who takes over the business, but the same rules about a trial period would apply.

How to claim

Your employer should make redundancy payments automatically if you are made redundant, but this may not always happen. In this case, request the payment in writing, although firstly you may need to take advice in case you have other claims on the employer, for example, if you have wages or holiday pay owing or you feel you have been unfairly dismissed. If the employer fails to pay, you can appeal to an employment tribunal (see *Introduction: Ten things you should know about claiming*).

If your employer has ceased trading due to going bust you will have to claim from the National Insurance Fund. Find out who has been appointed to sort out the employer's affairs - perhaps a trustee, a liquidator or a receiver. They should send you a form RP1 on which you can claim, if not ask for one. Send the form to the Redundancy Payments Office for the part of the country you live in (see *Useful addresses*). On this form you may also need to claim for unpaid wages and other money owed - see *In brief - if your employer goes bust.*

The Rent a Room Scheme: tax relief if you have a lodger at home

You may be better off claiming tax relief under this scheme if you have a lodger at home. For more information on tax reliefs and how to claim them, see *Appendix: Tax allowances and tax reliefs and your Tax Return - some general points.*

Qualification checklist

- The scheme only applies if you let rooms in your only or main home.
- You yourself must be living in the property.
- It doesn't matter if you have a mortgage on the home or you yourself are a tenant, but you will need to have the permission of the lender or landlord to let rooms out.
- You cannot claim under this Scheme and also claim relief for expenses (see *Letting out rooms: tax relief*).

> **Amount Box**
>
> If the income you receive is less than £4,250 over the year you will not have to pay tax on it, you just pay tax on any excess over this amount. So if your income is £6,000, you will have to pay tax on £1,750 (£6,000 - £4,250). It is only your gross income that counts here - you cannot deduct any expenses. If someone else living in the same house is letting out another room or you are jointly letting out room(s), the relief is split equally so the limit for each of you will be £2,125.

How to claim

If your income is less than the limit in the Amount box, all you have to do is tick the relevant box in the Land and Property supplementary pages of the Tax Return. You will have no tax to pay. If you have no other reason to fill in a Tax Return, the Inland Revenue are happy not to know about the income at all. If your income is above the limit you just pay tax on the excess but in that case you may be better off getting tax relief by claiming expenses - see *Letting out rooms: tax relief.*

Retirement Benefit: Graduated

This is a small extra benefit you may qualify for whether or not you are entitled to a Retirement Pension. The pension is taxable.

Amount box

	Weekly amount
For a man, for every £7.50 you contributed	9.21p
For a woman, for every £9.00 you contributed	9.21p
Age addition *An extra amount if you are 80 or over if you are not receiving a Retirement Pension*	25p

This pension does not come with an addition for a child or a spouse. If you are a widow, you can add half of your husband's entitlement to your own to work out your total amount. The same applies to your wife's contributions if you are a widower, if you qualify for Category A or Category B Retirement Pension. If you defer your claim beyond pension age you can get an increase, as for Retirement Pension: Category A (see the relevant chapter). Do be warned that you will not get an increase for the Category A Retirement Pension if you don't defer the Graduated Pension as well.

You can find out how your record stands, and what pension you are forecast to receive by asking the Inland Revenue Contributions Office for a pension forecast (see *Retirement Pension: Category A*).

Qualification checklist

- You paid National Insurance contributions between 6 April 1961 and 6 April 1975. If you did, you would normally have paid what were called 'graduated contributions'.
- You are aged 60 or over (woman) or 65 or over (man).

How to claim

See *Retirement Pension: Category A* as the procedure and *Useful addresses* is the same.

Retirement Pension: Category A

There are several types of state pension - this one is based on your own National Insurance contribution record.

Qualification checklist

- You are aged 60 and over (women) or aged 65 and over (men).
- In your working life you must have made sufficient National Insurance contributions in most of the tax years. Now you may have paid these, for example, as an employee or self-employed, but you will still qualify here if you didn't pay them but instead they were credited to you (because you were claiming another benefit at the time). If your National Insurance contributions are short, you may still get a reduced pension but it may not be too late to make up the difference by paying some contributions for previous years.
- Even though credits count, there is still a need for you to have had at least one tax year when you actually paid sufficient National Insurance contributions. However, you can ignore this stipulation if you have been receiving the long-term rate of Incapacity Benefit in at least one of the two years before you retire.

Two ways you can increase your pension

- If you do find out that you have a shortfall, it may be worthwhile making voluntary National Insurance contributions. This might improve your record sufficiently to enable you to get the full rate of pension or at least a higher rate than what you would have originally received. Take advice on this when you have got your pension forecast. Seeing a financial adviser may help because you may get a better return by investing money rather than making voluntary contributions. Anyway, you can only pay contributions in this way up to six years from the end of the tax year they were due, so if you are looking to make contributions for the year 1998/99, for example, you must do so by 5 April 2005.
- You can defer claiming your Retirement Pension and for every week you do this, the pension you eventually receive is increased by one seventh of 1 per cent. This means that if you defer your pension for five years (you cannot do it for more than five years), you will get just over 37 per cent extra each week when you do claim. However, it will not be as much as this if during the five years you claimed another contributory benefit such as Incapacity Benefit or graduated

Amount box

	Weekly amount
The pension for you	£75.50
Spouse or adult dependant *(provided he is not earning more than £53.95 - see below)*	£45.20
For the eldest child *If you are not getting Child Benefit for this child, the amount is increased to £11.35. If you are getting the lone parent rate of Child Benefit for the same child, the amount will be reduced by £7.65.*	£9.65
Other children	£11.35
Age Addition *You get this once you are over 80!!*	£0.25

The pension you receive for yourself and for your spouse or other adult dependant may be less than this if you have an incomplete National Insurance record, but any increase for a child would be unaffected. You can find out how your record stands and what pension you are forecast to receive by asking the Inland Revenue Contributions Office for a pension forecast - your local Inland Revenue Enquiry Office can supply you with a request form or you can apply online at www.inlandrevenue.gov.uk.

If you are forecast to get a reduced pension, it is probably because you have not paid enough contributions in enough tax years in your working life. If you miss a small number of tax years, your pension may not be affected. For example, you can miss up to five years if your working life lasts 41 or more years but if it lasts only up to 10 years, you can afford to miss only one year.

Retirement Pension. Before deciding to defer your claim, do take financial advice as you may be getting a better return by claiming and investing the money. Also, it is usually of no advantage to defer claiming if you intend to claim means-tested benefits as it will be assumed that you are getting a pension even if you are not.

- If you think deferring Retirement Pension is a good idea but you are already receiving it, you can de-retire! You have to notify your local social security office - they can provide you with a special form to do this.
- Any income you receive does not affect the pension for yourself.
- You can claim for a spouse or adult dependant - the rules and the earnings limit are the same as for Incapacity Benefit.

Working life

So how do you work out the length of your working life? Basically it is the number of tax years from the tax year in which you were 16 up to the tax year before you reach 60 (for a woman) or 65 (for a man). However, if you were 16 before 6 April 1948, it is deemed to have started on that date (unless you were paying the old style contributions before then). Total up the number and that's your working life - except if there are any tax years in which you claimed Home Responsibilities Protection, you can knock these off your total, as they don't count.

How to claim

About four months before you reach pensionable age, you will usually be sent a claim form (BR1). You will need to complete this form and send it to your local social security office together with a birth certificate or passport to prove your age. If you cannot get this evidence, contact the social security office or take advice. As an alternative, you can claim on the phone by contacting the Retirement Pensions Tele-claim Service (see *Useful addresses*).

If you have not received a form three months before you need the pension, contact your local social security office. For further information, contact the Pensions Information Line, the Department for Work and Pensions (Pensions Direct) or the Pensions Service (see *Useful addresses*).

Retirement Pension: Category A if you are divorced

What if you are divorced and you don't qualify for a Retirement Pension: Category A in your own right, or your pension will be reduced because your National Insurance record is poor? It is possible to claim a Retirement Pension based on your ex-spouse's record as well as your own.

Qualification checklist

- You are aged 60 and over (women) or aged 65 and over (men).
- You are divorced (it will not matter if your ex-spouse hasn't yet reached the above retirement ages).
- You would get a reduced Retirement Pension: Category A, or none at all, due to your poor National Insurance record and you are better off using your ex-spouse's record.

How to claim

See Retirement Pension: Category A as the procedure and Useful addresses are the same.

What if you're reading this chapter because you're thinking of getting divorced? If your spouse is still working and paying National Insurance you may receive more pension if you put off divorcing until they retire, unless you are getting remarried. Take advice.

Amount box

The amounts are as for Retirement Pension: Category A. If you apply for a pension forecast naming your ex-spouse and giving his National Insurance number, the calculation of your entitlement based on your and your ex-spouse's record will be made. Otherwise, take advice. What is looked at is your ex-spouse's record in his working life up until his divorce from you. This is compared to your record in either your own working life up to your divorce, or your working life only during the years you were married. Whichever is the higher will be the record that will be used to work out your pension.

If after all this your National Insurance contributions are still short, you may still get a reduced pension but you may not be too late to make your own record compare more favourably to your ex-spouse's by paying some contributions for previous years or deferring your retirement. See *Retirement Pension: Category A* for how to do these things.

Retirement Pension: Category B for a married woman

If you have a poor National Insurance record because you haven't been in paid employment for much of your working life, you may be able to claim this pension.

Amount box

	Weekly amount
The pension for you	£45.20
For the eldest child *If you are not getting Child Benefit for this child, the amount is increased to £11.35. If you are getting the lone parent rate of Child Benefit for the same child, the amount will be reduced by £7.65.*	£9.65
Other children	£11.35
Age Addition *You get this once you are over 80!!*	£0.25

The rules for claiming for a child are the same as for the Category A Retirement Pension. As for that pension, your pension may be reduced if your husband has an incomplete National Insurance record - see *Retirement Pension: Category A* on how to work out his working life and get a pension forecast. See also that chapter on deferring your pension and making voluntary contributions but in both cases for this Category B pension, your husband would have to do it. It may be worth considering whether you would be better off improving your own National Insurance record in this way and claiming a Category A pension in your own right instead.

Qualification checklist

- You are a married woman.
- You are 60 or over and your husband is aged 65 or over.
- Your husband's National Insurance record is good enough - see *Retirement Pension: Category A* as the rules here are the same except it's your husband's record you need to look at and not your own.

- Your husband is entitled to a Category A Retirement Pension. (Do note that if you claim this Category B pension, he will not be able to get an increase for you on his pension, nor for a child if you have one, if you claim for the child addition.)

How to claim

See *Retirement Pension: Category A* as the procedure and *Useful addresses* are the same.

Retirement Pension: Category B for a widow

If you don't qualify for a pension in your own right due to your poor National Insurance record, you may be able to claim for this benefit.

Qualification checklist

- You were 60 or over when your husband died.
- Alternatively, you will qualify if you were a widow immediately before you reached the age of 60 and you were claiming Widow's Pension. (Widow's Pensions are only available where the husband died on or before 9 April 2001).
- If you would have been getting Widow's Pension but it was suspended because you were living with a new partner, you will still qualify. However, if you remarry prior to the age of 60, you will lose the Widow's Pension altogether, which in turn means that you will not qualify for the Category B pension as you will not be a widow immediately before you are 60!
- Once you qualify, you cannot be disqualified if you are living with a new partner or if you remarry.
- Your husband's National Insurance record is good enough - see *Retirement Pension: Category A* as the rules here are the same except it's your husband's record you need to look at and not your own.
- If your husband died of an industrial injury or disease, the above rule about National Insurance is ignored. The injury or disease must have been a cause of death, but not necessarily the direct cause or the only cause. If you are claiming on these grounds, the social security office will normally consider your case as they would if he had been claiming Industrial Disablement Benefit. See the chapter on that benefit.

Amount box

	Weekly amount
The pension for you	£75.50
For the eldest child *If you are not getting Child Benefit for this child, the amount is increased to £11.35. If you are getting the lone parent rate of Child Benefit for the same child, the amount will be reduced by £7.65.*	£9.65
Other children	£11.35
Age Addition *You get this once you are over 80!!*	£0.25

The rules for claiming for a child are the same as for Category A Retirement Pension. Your pension may be reduced if your husband has an incomplete National Insurance record (more likely if he died before he retired). See *Retirement Pension: Category A* on how to work out his working life and get a pension forecast. However, the reduction will not be made if an industrial accident or disease led to his death. See also that chapter on making voluntary contributions as you can pay them on behalf of your husband after his death.

Your pension might also be reduced if you were receiving Widow's Pension at the reduced rate because of your age when widowed. A table of these reductions is in the chapter on Bereavement Allowance.

How to claim

You should be paid automatically when you're 65 if you've been receiving Widowed Mother's Allowance or Widows Benefit. However, you may want to claim earlier (when you are 60 or over) in which case, see Retirement Pension: Category A as the procedure and *Useful addresses* are the same.

If you remarry or live with a new partner you are not disqualified once you are receiving it, although remarriage may stop you getting it in the first place.

Retirement Pension: Category B for a widower

If you do not qualify for a pension in your own right due to your poor National Insurance record, you may be able to claim on your wife's contributions, if you are a widow.

Qualification checklist

- Your wife died on or after 6 April 1979.
- Your wife was 60 or over when she died, and you were 65 or over.
- Your wife's National Insurance record is good enough - see *Retirement Pension: Category A* as the rules here are the same except its your wife's record you need to look at and not your own.
- Once you qualify, you cannot be disqualified if you are living with a new partner or if you remarry.

Amount box

	Weekly amount
The pension for you	£75.50
For the eldest child *If you are not getting Child Benefit for this child, the amount is increased to £11.35. If you are getting the lone parent rate of Child Benefit for the same child, the amount will be reduced by £7.65.*	£9.65
Other children	£11.35
Age Addition *You get this once you are over 80!!*	£0.25

The rules for claiming for a child are the same as for Retirement Pension: Category A.

As for that pension, your pension may be reduced if your wife has an incomplete National Insurance record. See *Retirement Pension: Category A* on how to work out her working life and get a pension forecast. See also that chapter on making voluntary contributions as you can pay them on behalf of your wife after her death.

How to claim

See *Retirement Pension: Category A* as the procedure and *Useful addresses* are the same. If you remarry or live with a new partner, your pension will not be affected once you are receiving it.

Retirement Pension: Category D if you are 80 or over

Other Retirement Pensions are related to your National Insurance contribution record. If this has been a problem for you, when you reach 80 you can at least get this pension in your own right.

Qualification checklist

- You are aged 80 or over.
- You were resident in Britain on the day you reached 80, and you have been resident for a period of at least 10 years in any continuous period of 20 years before you reached 80.
- You are entitled to no other retirement pension, or if you are, the amount you are entitled to is less than the amount of this pension (see *Amount box*).

How to claim

If you are already receiving another retirement pension, you should automatically be paid this pension (if you are better off receiving it) instead of your old pension. If you don't get it, see the chapter *Retirement Pension: Category A* as the procedure for claiming and *Useful addresses* are the same.

Amount box

	Weekly amount
The pension for you	£45.45

This pension does not come with an addition for a child or a spouse.

Retirement Pension: The State Second Pension (S2P)

From 6 April 2002, if you are entitled to an additional pension, you will be claiming under a new scheme called the State Second Pension (S2P). This takes over from

Amount box

The calculation of your S2P entitlement is complicated so take advice if you want to do it yourself. Alternatively, if you ask for a pensions forecast from the Inland Revenue Contributions Office (see *Retirement Pension: Category A*), you can find out how your record stands and what pension you are forecast to receive.

Generally speaking, your entitlement depends on how many tax years in your working life you were earning enough to pay National Insurance contributions, and your 'earnings factor' for each of these years, i.e. the actual amount of earnings on which you were paying National Insurance. From 2002/03 onwards, years when you are not earning may also increase your entitlement - see the *Qualification checklist*. In addition, provided you have worked and actually paid National Insurance contributions for one tenth of your working life, years when you receive Incapacity Benefit may also help increase the amount to which you are entitled (see *Retirement Pension: Category A* about working life).

'SERPS' (State Earnings Related Pension). The amount you are entitled to will depend on your earnings and other circumstances in tax years from 1978/79.

Qualification checklist

- You are aged 60 or over (woman) or 65 or over (man).
- In at least one tax year from 1978/79 you have earned enough as an employee (not self-employed) to pay National Insurance contributions.
- However, for S2P you cannot include any tax year where you or your employer had agreed to 'contract out' of the scheme. This may have happened if you agreed to contribute to an alternative pension scheme provided by your employer.
- Alternatively, you may qualify if in at least one tax year from 2002/03 you were either receiving Child Benefit for a child under six, or you were entitled to Invalid Care Allowance, or you qualified for Home Responsibilities Protection because you were caring for a sick or disabled person. This can only apply to you if you are claiming S2P on 6 April 2003 or after.
- If you are a married woman with a poor National Insurance record, you may be claiming Category B Retirement Pension on your husband's earnings. In order

to receive S2P in this instance, the above will have to apply to your husband instead.

- If you are a widow or widower, you may be claiming Widowed Parent's Allowance or Category B Retirement Pension for widows or widowers. Again, to get S2P you will usually be claiming using your spouse's record rather than your own.

How to claim

See *Retirement Pension: Category A*, as the procedure and *Useful addresses* are the same.

If you are also getting a Retirement Pension, you will be paid this benefit at the same time.

School clothing

School uniforms and other clothing needed for school can be expensive, but there are schemes to help meet the bills.

Qualification checklist

- You have to be a school student under the age of 18.
- Whether or not you qualify beyond this will depend on the policy of the body you are applying to and these vary greatly across the country. It is more likely you will qualify if you live on a low income or your family has special circumstances.

How to apply (and to whom)

The starting point is your Local Education Authority (LEA). They have discretion to assist with the cost of school clothing for pupils in county, voluntary and maintained special schools and colleges for further education and sixth form colleges. This can include uniform and non-uniform clothes, shoes and sports kit. You will need to find out their policy on who they will help and for what items, and what procedures they have for applying. Some LEAs restrict help to school uniform only. If you feel the help is inadequate, and expensive school uniform is compulsory, take advice about complaining to the LEA.

You could also try the governing body or Parents' Association of the school or college itself. Any help they give should be publicised in the information given to parents about the school, or you could ask the school head or a senior staff member. They may run a second-hand uniform shop where the clothing can be bought cheaply by any parent, or they may keep a special stock of second -hand clothing for pupils who fall within its criteria for help. A parent can find out what help is available from the Parents' Association or head teacher.

There may also be a charitable trust in your area which can help meet school uniform costs. Their criteria will vary, for example, they may say that you have to live in a particular area or belong to a certain religious faith.

If a school student or pupil is disabled and the parent or guardian looking after them is on Income Support or Income Based Job Seeker's Allowance, it may be possible for them to claim a Community Care Grant from the Social Fund to help with the cost of school clothing (see *Community Care Grant*).

Payment

The method of payment varies. Some LEAs and charitable trusts give the help as cash grants, whilst others give vouchers to be used at local shops or give actual items of clothing. Some pay a one-off grant when the pupil starts school, whilst others pay regular grants as the pupil grows and needs new clothing.

School transport

You may qualify for free transport - or financial help with transport - for your child to travel to and from school. Your child may be able to claim a cycling allowance. Local Education Authorities (LEAs) have a duty to provide this for pupils up to the age of 16 if they consider it is necessary to enable the pupil to get the nearest suitable school. This applies even if the nearest suitable school is in a different local authority area or if it is an independent school.

Qualification checklist

LEAs' policies vary but you are likely to qualify if your child is under 16 and either of the following applies:

- Your child has an illness, or a disability, which makes it difficult or impossible for him to walk to school.

- You live beyond 'walking distance' of the school - this means up to two miles for pupils under the age of 8 or up to three miles for 8 to 16 year-olds. It doesn't matter that he may not actually walk to school - it's the distance that counts. Walking distance is measured by the nearest available route and is generally taken to be door-to-door. However, you may not qualify if you choose a school beyond walking distance when there is (in the eyes of the LEA) a nearer suitable school. However, this does not apply to a voluntary school, for example, a church school, where they should pay if the school is beyond walking distance, even if there is a nearer non-church school available.
- You live within 'walking distance' of the school but, without free transport, your child cannot reasonably be expected to get to the school. The LEA must look at such factors as the age of the pupil, the safety of the route (for example, whether there are well lit pavements), how long the pupil has to wait for public transport, and whether the pupil has particular medical or mobility needs.

How to claim

Contact the LEA for details of their school transport policies. They are legally required to publish them annually and the school may supply you with a copy. This should set out who qualifies and how to claim.

How you receive the free transport

The LEA or school governing body will provide its own transport, hire coaches or provide free bus or train passes for use on public transport. A travelling allowance may be paid to your child if they provide their own transport, for example, a cycle allowance. You may receive a car allowance if you take your child to school or to a pick-up point agreed by the LEA.

If you qualify, make sure you get payment for the whole journey. Usually, this will mean from the bus stop, railway station or pick-up point nearest to your home to the one nearest the school.

If your child has an assisted place at an independent school, you can get help from the Department for Education and Skills (DfES) if your income is below a certain amount - see *Useful addresses*. Take advice.

If you do not qualify

The LEA may be willing to pay part of the travelling costs under its discretionary powers, so you could enquire about this. If all else fails your child may be allowed to travel on spare seats on the school bus for an agreed charge.

If your child's school is a city technology college, ask if you could apply to the governing body for help.

Self-employment expenses: tax relief

Income you receive as a self-employed person is taxable but you can claim tax relief on expenses you incur. This will be the case whether you are running a business full time, or whether you are doing occasional work in your spare time. For more information on tax reliefs and how to claim them see *Appendix: Tax allowances and tax reliefs and your Tax Return - some general points.*

Qualification checklist

- You have to be genuinely self-employed. In some cases, you may think you are self-employed but the Inland Revenue take the view that you are an employee. For example, you are self-employed if you control how your business is run - that is you decide what work you take on, where you do the work and what hours you keep. Take advice.

Expenses for which you can claim tax relief

Self-employment tax relief is a big subject - take advice for more detail. If you are operating as a partnership or a limited company, again take advice as other complications arise which are beyond the scope of this book.

Certain expenses qualify but it is hard to set out hard and fast rules as different types of businesses qualify for different expenses and to a different extent. In claiming you have to justify the expense within the context of your own line of work. Here is some broad guidance:

- A basic capital allowance for plant and machinery, cars and vans, information and communications technology, and for buying in the necessary know-how. You'll need to take advice on what proportion of such expenditure qualifies for tax relief - it will depend on the type of equipment, whether you are in an Enterprise Zone, the size of your business, etc. Any capital expenditure must be wholly or partly for business use to qualify.

- Normally allowed are employment costs (including wages, National Insurance, pension costs, other insurances and training); premises costs such as rent, rates, heating and lighting; general maintenance and repairs; administration expenses such as postage, stationery, telephone, printing, trade or professional journals, legal and professional fees, motoring expenses, travel and subsistence, advertising, promotion, bad debts - that is items you have invoiced for but no longer expect to get paid, interest and other fees on a business loan or overdraft, bank charges.

- If part of your home is used exclusively for business, you can claim for a proportion of your home costs based on how much of your home you use. So if you use one room, you could claim a proportion based on the floor area of the room as a percentage of the floor area for the whole home. In this, case you can even include a percentage of your mortgage interest.

How to claim

You claim the relief when you declare your profit from self-employment in your Tax Return, in the self-employed supplementary pages. So if the income you received in the year was £4,500 and your expenses amounted to £2,500, you can declare profits of £2,000 (£4,500 - £2,500). You won't actually need to set out your expenses in the Tax Return if your total letting income is less than £15,000 over the year, but it's best to keep your own record in case the Inland Revenue decide to check up on you. If your income is more than this limit, there is a space in the Tax Return where you have to list the expenses.

If you are a farmer, artist, writer or other creative worker, the Inland Revenue accepts that your income may vary substantially from year to year so you can ask them to allow you to be taxed on the average of your profits.

If you make a loss in any year, you may still be able to claim tax relief. You can ask the Inland Revenue to either set it against previous tax years, or for it to be set against future profits, or alternatively for it to be set against other income you are paying tax on, for example, if you also work as an employee. You can do this even if your business is more or less a hobby or sideline, provided you are seriously intending to make a profit. Take advice.

Social Services Direct Payments

Many local council Social Services Departments are now running direct payment schemes and if not, they have probably got one in the pipeline. The schemes are designed so that instead of receiving community care services from Social Services, you receive the money instead, and then use it to purchase the services you need.

Qualification checklist

Each council will have their own rules, but these national guidelines must apply:

- You are a disabled person (in Scotland, any person who requires community care services).
- You have been assessed by the Social Services Department as needing community care services.
- You are aged 16 or over.
- You are able to manage payments (alone or with assistance).
- If all these do not apply to you, you may still be able to claim if you are a carer or parent of someone it does apply to.

How to claim

Apply to your local council Social Services Department for an assessment of your community care needs, if you haven't already had one. You can apply for some or all of these needs to be met by means of direct payments rather than the council providing the services themselves. You may be able to include transport and equipment costs if the council agree. If you are a carer, you can apply for payments for the disabled person you are caring for to be accommodated in a care home for up to four weeks in a year, and it should be possible to apply for vouchers for short-term breaks from caring. You cannot use direct payments to pay a spouse or partner or other close relative living in the same household, although you may be able to use them to employ a relative living elsewhere, or someone who isn't a close relative living with you.

For further advice contact the council or National Centre for Independent Living or your local independent living organisation, or in Scotland, the Scottish Executive (see *Useful addresses*).

If payments are agreed, the council will want to make checks every so often to ensure the money is being spent on the care you are assessed as needing. You may be asked to repay money if this isn't the case.

If you apply to the council and they say that they are not running a direct payment scheme, take advice, because they are still obliged to consider your case on its merits.

Amount box

The council must meet the reasonable cost of the services to meet your assessed needs.

Statutory Maternity Pay (SMP)

If you are expecting a baby, your employer may be obliged to pay you whilst you are off work. Your employer may be more generous than this, but they must at least pay SMP.

Qualification checklist

- You must be 16 or over.
- You are an employee, and by the time you are into the 15th week before the baby is due to be born, you have worked for the same employer for 26 weeks continuously, part-time or full-time.
- You are pregnant, expecting the baby within the next 11 weeks or you've just had your baby.
- Your earnings on average are equal to, or above, the current weekly National Insurance low earnings limit - see *Amount box*.
- If you are dismissed after the 15th week before the baby is due, or indeed whilst you are receiving SMP, your employer is still obliged to pay you. Indeed, you may still be able to claim if you are dismissed earlier - take advice. However, if you resign you will not be entitled, unless you did so because of your pregnancy.

Amount box

Higher rate	90% of your average gross weekly earnings (that is, before tax and National Insurance contributions are deducted), with a minimum of £75.

This is paid for the first six weeks of maternity leave.

Lower rate	£75

Paid for the next twelve weeks.

The National Insurance Lower Earnings Limit is £75 per week.

Some employers have maternity policies that pay more than SMP. See your written statement of employment particulars (your contract of employment) or staff handbook, or ask your employer.

How to claim

The above written statement of employment particulars or staff handbook should set out your employer's policy and procedures on claiming, but here are the basics that apply to everyone.

You have some choice on when to start receiving your SMP, baby permitting! The earliest you can start getting paid is the 11th week before the baby is due. The latest is the week after the week when the baby is born. You lose this choice, though, if you are sick with a pregnancy related illness. If this happens in the six weeks before the baby is due, your SMP will start the week following the week you became sick. If you are sick with a non-pregnancy related illness, you can claim Statutory Sick Pay until the week the baby is due.

Claiming from your employer

You will need to give your employer 21 days' notice in writing of when you intend to stop work, or if this is impossible as much notice as practicable. You do not have to say whether or not you intend to return to work later. If the baby is born before the date you said you wanted to stop work, you will need to give the employer another notice in writing - within 21 days of the birth - giving the date the baby was born and the date from which you have now stopped work! You are still entitled to SMP if the baby was stillborn so long as the birth was after the 24th week of pregnancy.

You will also need to give your employer evidence of the expected date of birth (MAT B1) available from your doctor or midwife. Do this up to three weeks after you start receiving SMP (if you do this later you have to have good cause). If the baby is born before you start claiming SMP, you will also need to supply a birth certificate.

Payment

SMP is paid for 18 weeks, the first six weeks at the higher rate, then the remaining 12 weeks at the lower rate. The employer will usually make the payments in the same way and at the same time as your wages.

Statutory Sick Pay (SSP)

If you are an employee your employer is usually obliged to make a payment to you even if you cannot work due to sickness.

Qualification checklist

- You are an employee. It doesn't matter how long you have been employed but you don't qualify if you have a fixed term contract of three months or less. (However, you will qualify if within eight weeks of this contract you are employed on another such contract and the length of both contracts added together is 13 or more weeks.)
- You are aged 16 to 65.
- You are incapable of doing your job because of sickness or disability.
- If you not actually incapable yourself, you can qualify if you are treated as such, for example, if you are under medical observation for being a carrier of an infectious disease, or you have recently been in contact with someone who has one.
- The days for which you are claiming SSP are days when you would normally work if you were not sick. These are called 'qualifying days'. If you work a complicated shift pattern, you and your employer can agree which days count for this purpose. Payment does not start until you have been sick for three qualifying days.
- Your earnings on average are equal to or above the current National Insurance low earnings limit (see *Amount box*). The average is usually based on the two months immediately prior to your last payday, unless you haven't been working for the employer that long, in which case a shorter period is used or an estimate of future earnings.
- You do not usually get SSP if you were receiving Incapacity Benefit within the past eight weeks. In this case, you should reclaim Incapacity Benefit.
- You cannot get SSP whilst you qualify for Statutory Maternity Pay or Maternity Allowance and even if you don't qualify for these, you cannot get it if you are within six weeks of the expected date of childbirth and are incapable of work due in part to the pregnancy.

How to claim

Your employer should get ready to pay you when you notify them that you will be absent from work due to sickness. In doing this, you should follow the employer's staff sickness policy. If you don't do this, the employer may refuse to pay you and may subject you to disciplinary proceedings. The policy should appear in your written statement of employment particulars (your contract of employment) or staff handbook. If not, ask your employer. If, for some reason, you can't get this information, the law says at the very least you should notify your employer in writing on or before the seventh qualifying day of sickness, or later if this is not practicable.

When you notify your employer of your sickness, you can enclose a medical certificate if you have one but you don't have to have one until you have been sick for seven days. After that, you must send in a medical certificate. Whatever type you provide - say from a doctor, an osteopath or a chiropractor - it is up to the employer to decide whether to accept it. Your employer may still decide not to pay you SSP because they feel you are capable of working. If this happens, take advice.

Amount box

The weekly rate is £63.25, although it can be paid for periods of less than a week. In this case, your entitlement will be this rate divided by the number of qualifying days you have in a week.

However, some employers have sickness schemes that pay more than SSP. See your written statement of employment particulars (your contract of employment) or staff handbook, or ask your employer.

The National Insurance low earnings limit is £75.

Payment

The employer usually pays SSP in the same way, and at the same time as you would normally get your wages.

SSP will be paid for a maximum of 28 weeks provided you keep to your employer's procedures - such as sending in medical certificates - but not for the first three days. If you make a fresh claim within eight weeks of a previous claim, you do not have to wait three days but the previous claim will be included in these 28 weeks.

Vitamin drops or tablets - free of charge

You may qualify for free vitamin drops or tablets if you are pregnant or have a child:

Qualification checklist

One of the following has to apply:

- You are pregnant or you are breastfeeding a baby under the age of one, and you, or your partner, receive Income Support or Income Based Job Seeker's Allowance.
- Your child or children qualify if they are under the age of five and you, or your partner, receive Income Support or Income Based Job Seeker's Allowance.

Amount box

If you are pregnant, or if you are claiming for a child, you are entitled to 20ml of vitamin drops every 13 weeks. If you are a breastfeeding mother, you can have the same amount of drops or you can have 90 tablets.

How to claim

Claim from your local child health or maternity clinic, showing proof that you are receiving one of the benefits above.

War Disablement Pension and other allowances

You may qualify for this pension if you have a disability caused or made worse by service in HM Armed Forces whether in war or peacetime. If your accident or illness occurred many years ago, it is worth claiming if you are still suffering from the effects.

Qualification checklist

- You must have an injury or condition which was caused or made worse by service in HM Armed Forces at any time. This includes service in the Home Guard, Nursing and Auxiliary Services, the Ulster Defence Regiment (from 31 March 1970 only), the Territorial Army and the Cadets.
- You can claim for any medical condition provided you can show a link between that condition and your service.
- You do not have to have been involved in war or active service when the injury or condition was caused, for example, you may have been playing sport on the base or you may have suffered an illness during service that has done permanent damage. This could mean, for example, an ear infection causing hearing loss, or a disease such as Multiple Sclerosis or Hodgkin's Disease, or a mental or psychological condition such as post traumatic stress disorder.

- You could have had an existing condition made worse by service.
- You may also be able to claim for certain illnesses or injuries sustained whilst serving in the Naval Auxiliary Services, Coastguard or Merchant Navy during the First World War or the Second World War, or later conflicts in the Gulf, the Falklands, Suez or South Korea. Being held prisoner in any of these situations will also count.
- If you became disabled as a civilian, you can claim but only for physical injuries or diseases arising from the Second World War as a result of enemy action or combating the enemy. The same applies if you were a Civil Defence Volunteer carrying out your duties.
- If you are a dependant of someone whose death has been caused or hastened by one of the above, you may also be able to claim a war pension.
- If you were a Prisoner of War in the Far East during the Second World War, you can claim a lump sum separate from the Disablement Pension. You may have been in the Forces, or a civilian, and in some cases a member of the colonial forces. If you are a widow or widower of someone who was in this situation, you can claim if they hadn't been paid themselves.
- You cannot qualify if you are claiming Industrial Disablement Allowance for the same disablement.

Additional allowances

In addition to the pension, you can claim extra allowances as follows:

- **War Pensioner's Mobility Supplement:** Similar qualifying rules as for higher rate Disability Living Allowance, but there is no upper age limit. You cannot be paid this allowance at the same time. Paid if your walking difficulty is caused at least in part by your pensioned disablement. This must be 40 per cent or more.
- **Constant Attendance Allowance:** For the rules on whether you qualify, see *Industrial Disablement Benefit* as the same applies.
- **Exceptionally Severe Disablement Allowance:** For the rules on whether you qualify, see *Industrial Disablement Benefit* as the same applies.
- **Unemployability Supplement:** Paid if you are assessed as at least 60 per cent disabled. You have to be under 65 when you claim but you can

continue to receive it after that age. You cannot get this at the same time as Incapacity Benefit or any Retirement Pension, but Standard Second Pension (S2P) and Graduated Retirement Pension can be paid on top. You are allowed to work up to 16 hours and earn up to £3,423 per year without this affecting the benefit, so long as your GP approves the work.

- **Allowance for Lowered Standard of Occupation:** Paid if you are at least 40 per cent disabled if you cannot follow your normal occupation or do work of an equivalent standard. Again, you have to claim before you are 65, but you can then keep receiving it after 65. This allowance plus your basic War Pension cannot add up to more than the rate for 100 per cent rate pension, so if it comes to more, the total will be reduced to that level. This can be paid as well as Incapacity Benefit and Retirement Allowance. You cannot get the allowance at the same time as Unemployability Supplement but you can get it on top of Incapacity Benefit or Retirement Pensions. Take advice as you may have a choice on what best to claim in your circumstances - contact the Veterans Agency.

- **Severe Disablement Occupational Allowance:** Paid if you get the two highest rates of constant Attendance Allowance but you still work, and Comforts Allowance is paid if you get Unemployability and/or Constant Attendance Allowance.

- **Comforts Allowance:** Paid if you get Unemployability Supplement and/or Constant Attendance Allowance.

- **Treatment Allowance:** Available to you if you have suffered a loss of earnings due to having treatment because of your disablement. It is paid on top of your other allowances.

- **Clothing allowance:** Paid if you get exceptional wear and tear on your clothing due to your disability.

How to claim

The following all have to be claimed separately: War Disablement Pension, War Pensioner's Mobility Supplement, Constant Attendance Allowance, and Unemployability Supplement, Allowance for lowered standard of occupation, Clothing Allowance and Treatment Allowance, and the special payment for Far East Prisoners of War. You can claim by phoning the Veterans Agency who will take certain details from you such as your service and medical details and send you the relevant claim packs. You can also get packs from your local Veterans Welfare Office, or print off forms from the Veterans Agency website at www.veteransagency.mod.uk.

If your disablement occurred as a result of you being in the services, you can claim any time but backdating is only allowed in certain circumstances, and then only for three years. If you claim after seven years of leaving the service, it may be more difficult for you to prove your disablement is linked to the actual service. Take advice. Civilians usually have to claim within three months but exceptions can be made.

In processing your claims the Veterans Agency will check your service record if relevant, then arrange for you to be medically examined, or with some allowances you can choose to fill in a self-assessment claim pack instead.

Payment

For War Disablement Pension, it is possible you may be given a provisional disability assessment for a fixed time period because the medical examiner considers that your condition has not yet settled down, and might get worse or better. Before the end of the time period, you will be invited for a further medical so that a final assessment can be made. Your assessment should include psychological effects of the accident or illness as these may affect your disability.

Depending on the nature of your disability, your final assessment may be for a limited period or for life. If, in your case, it's a limited period and you are still disabled, you will need to apply for a renewal of benefit. In order to avoid a gap in payments, you should do this about three months before the fixed period expires. If you don't renew your claim because you feel better and then later you get worse again, in this case you can reapply and you will not have to wait for another 15 weeks. The War Pensioner's Mobility Supplement will usually be paid direct to Motability if you use that scheme to buy or hire a car. See *In brief*.

Extra help you can get

Extra grants may be paid so contact the Veterans Agency for further details. Here are some examples:

- Hospital treatment expenses can be claimed. These can include patients' travel costs, subsistence or loss of earnings incurred when attending hospital. In some circumstances, visitors can claim travel expenses also. Private treatment may be paid for if not available free on the NHS.

- Up to £750 can be paid for small adaptations to the home.
- If you need skilled nursing care because of your pensioned disability, up to £431 per week can be paid (£491 in London) for your stay in a nursing home so long as this is not already being paid for by Social Services Department. A higher rate may be paid if you are faced with a higher fee and there is no other nursing home available that can meet your needs.
- You may be able to claim for respite fees to give your carer a break.

Amount box

The amount of pension you will get will depend on the severity of your injuries, whether you have difficulties in walking, whether you need to have someone to care for you, your age, your job prospects following the injuries and your rank when you were injured. Take advice or contact the Veterans Agency. If you were a Far East Prisoner of War, the lump sum you can claim is £10,000.

War Widow's or Widower's Pension

If your spouse died and was receiving a War Disablement Pension, or would have qualified for one, you may be able to claim a pension. War widowers should take note that until April 2002 it was more difficult to qualify but since then all has changed and you should certainly claim. It doesn't matter if you were turned down before under the old rules - the new rules give you the same rights as widows.

Qualification checklist

- Your spouse's death was due to, or substantially hastened by, an illness or injury for which he was receiving either a War Disablement Pension, Constant Attendance Allowance (or would have been if they were not in hospital) or Unemployability Supplement (provided his pensionable disablement was 80 per cent).
- If on reading the chapter on War Disablement Pension you now think that he should have claimed, take advice, as you may still be able to get a pension.
- In some circumstances, if you were not married to the deceased, you may be able to claim if you were living with him at the time of death and looking after his child.

Amount box

You qualify for the higher rate if you are a widow of an officer above the rank of Major or equivalent, or you are aged 40 or over, or under 40 but getting an allowance for a child, or not able to financially support yourself. Otherwise, you will get the lower rate until you reach 40.

The amount depends on your circumstances and the rank of your spouse in the Forces when you were widowed, for example, you may qualify for a children's allowance, a rent allowance (up to £34.80), or an extra allowance for other dependants. There is also a War Orphan's Pension for children. Take advice. The Supplementary Pension is £59.95, and the Temporary Widow's Pension is paid at the same rate as the War Disablement Pension that your spouse was getting.

How to claim

You can claim by phoning the Veterans Agency. They may take certain details from you, such as your spouse's service and medical details, and send you a claim pack. You can also get a pack from your local Veterans Welfare Office, or print off a form from the Veterans Agency website at www.veteransagency.mod.uk.

Claim any time, but backdating is only allowed in certain circumstances, and then only for three years.

If your spouse was receiving Constant Attendance Allowance or Unemployability Supplement at the time of death you will automatically be paid the Temporary Widow's or Widower's Allowance for 26 weeks to bide you over while you receive a claim for a pension. You will receive a supplementary pension if your late spouse's service ended before 31 March 1973.

Entitlement stops if you remarry or live with someone as a partner, and you cannot get War Widow's/Widower's Pension as well as a Widow's Pension or Widowed Parent's Allowance, but you can also get Retirement Pension and Incapacity Benefit.

Widowed Parent's Allowance

If you have been widowed and you have children to bring up, this is the allowance you may qualify for.

Qualification checklist

- You are a widow or widower because your spouse died on or after 9 April 2001.
- You were living with your spouse, or if you were living apart, this was only meant to be a temporary arrangement (i.e. you had intended to get back together again).
- You are under age 60 (widow) or 65 (widower).
- However, if your spouse died before 9 April 2001 and you have yet to claim, you may still qualify. (If you are a widow, you would be claiming the old benefit Widowed Mother's Allowance.) Take advice.
- In their working life, up until death, your late spouse must have made sufficient National Insurance contributions in most of the tax years, either paid or credited.
- Despite saying above that credits count, there is still a need for him to have had at least one tax year when he actually paid sufficient National Insurance contributions, although you can ignore this stipulation if he had been receiving long-term rate Incapacity Benefit in at least one of the two years before he died.
- The National Insurance record is irrelevant if your spouse died as a result of an accident or disease directly or indirectly connected to work - see *Industrial Disablement Benefit.*
- You are entitled to Child Benefit for at least one child or if you are a widow pregnant by your late husband (or you were living with him and are pregnant as a result of IVF or artificial insemination carried out before he died).
- You are not living with a person of the opposite sex as a partner.
- Normally you cannot qualify if you were criminally responsible for his death, but take advice as this is a complicated area.
- If your marriage was polygamous, you may not qualify, but take advice, as the law is complex on this. The same may apply if you were divorced in another country then remarried, as it is possible that the UK may not recognise your divorce.

Amount box

Basic allowance	£75.50
Increase for eldest child *If you are not getting Child Benefit for this child, the amount is increased to £11.35.*	£9.65
Increase for each other child	£11.35

You may get less than these amounts if your ex-spouse's National Insurance record is poor, but not poor enough for you not to qualify at all. You may be able to improve the record by making voluntary contributions - see *Retirement Pension: Category A* for how to do this.

In addition to Widowed Parent's Allowance, you may qualify for an additional pension related to your late spouse's earnings; see *Retirement Pension: The State Second Pension (S2P).*

How to claim

You can make a claim on form BB1, the same form with which you claim Widowed Parent's Allowance and Bereavement Allowance. This is available on the DWP website at www.dwp.gov.uk or from your local social security office. You will usually need to supply your marriage certificate and your spouse's death certificate, or the extra certificate you get when you register the death - the Certificate of Registration or Notification of Death. If your spouse has gone missing and you think he is dead, take advice. If you get a court to declare presumption of death, this will usually be enough to get the DWP to pay, but otherwise they may only pay if there is strong evidence of the death. Otherwise, you may have to wait until seven years have elapsed, DWP will then start paying if they are satisfied that during that time there is no evidence to suggest the spouse is alive.

You will get paid so long as you qualify as above but if you find a new partner, your benefit will be suspended. However, you can apply for it to be reinstated if you split up but not if you marry then separate!

Winter fuel payments

This is an annual lump sum payment to help with your fuel costs in the winter.

Qualification checklist

- You are aged 60 or over in the week beginning on the third Monday in September.
- You will not qualify if you are living with a partner who is receiving Income Support or Income Based Job Seeker's Allowance and is himself entitled to a winter fuel payment. You will also not qualify if you have been receiving treatment as a hospital patient (but not an outpatient) or if you receive Income Support or Income Based Job Seeker's Allowance whilst in a residential or nursing home.

Back payments

Whilst reading this, you realise that you should have claimed a payment in previous years, you can claim now but only for three particular winters where the Government were held by the European Court to have restricted eligibility. These are:

- The winter of 1997/98: you would have to have qualified in the week of 5-11 January 1998 and you would be entitled to £20 (or £10 if you were a couple as above).
- The winter of 1998/99: you would have to have qualified in the week of 9-15 November 1998 and you would be entitled to the same amount.
- The winter of 1999/2000: you would have to have qualified in the week of 20-26 September 1999 and you would be entitled to £100 (or £50 if you were a couple as above).

Amount box

If you live on your own	£200
If you share accommodation with someone and you receive Income Support or Income Based Job Seeker's Allowance	£100 between you
If you share accommodation with someone and you receive neither of these benefits, and you are both 60 or over	£100 each

How to claim

Normally you are automatically paid if you were paid the previous year, or if you are getting the other above-mentioned benefits in the week you qualify. Otherwise you will need to claim by 31 March following that week, but do claim before the qualifying week if you want to be paid by Christmas. You can get a claim form from the local social security office or by phoning the Winter Fuel Payment helpline (see *Useful addresses*) or from the DWP website at www.dwp.gov.uk.

You will need a special claim form to claim the back payments.

Payment

You are paid as an extra amount with your other benefit payment, otherwise by cheque.

Working Families' Tax Credit (WFTC)

Whether you are a single parent or living as a couple, you can claim this benefit if you are bringing up a family and are finding your finances are stretched. It may assist you in topping up your earnings and allows for childcare expenses. Any claim you make now will be paid up until 7 April 2003 as the benefit will be replaced from that date by the Working Tax Credit and the Child Tax Credit (see the chapters on these benefits).

Qualification checklist

You, or your partner if you have one, must qualify in the following manner:

- You work as an employee or are self-employed for 16+ hours a week on average.
- Regarding averages, some weeks you may do less than 16 hours, but you must have actually worked 16 hours in either the week you claim or one of the two preceding weeks, or at least you are expected to work 16+ hours in the week following your claim.
- There is an exception to this last point. If you are on maternity leave (provided you are receiving Statutory Maternity Leave or Maternity Allowance), you must have worked 16+ hours before you went on maternity leave.

Amount box

Your entitlement will be made up of different individual tax credits depending on your circumstances.

- If your income is less than £94.50 (called the 'applicable amount') you will receive the maximum WFTC. In order to work out what this is in your case, add together the credits that apply to you.
- If your income is more than £94.50, you can work out your entitlement by adding together the credits that apply to you, then from this total deduct 55% of the excess. For example, if you calculate that your maximum entitlement is £124.55 and your income is £130.50 per week, this is £36 greater than the 'applicable amount'. 55% of this £36 is £19.80, so you will need to deduct £19.80 from the maximum entitlement = £104.75. This £104.75 will be your entitlement.

If you have a partner or spouse	£60
If you are a lone parent	£60
For each child aged under 16 (not paid if the child has his own income above this amount)	£26.45
For each child aged 16 -18 (in full-time education) (not paid if the child has his own income above this amount)	£27.20
If you and/or your partner works 30 + hours per week	£11.65
If you have a child for whom you are receiving Disability Living Allowance (DLA) or who is registered blind	£35.50
Alternative to the above if you receive the DLA care component at the higher rate for the child	£46.75
If you or your partner receive DLA care component at the higher rate	£16.25
Childcare Tax Credit - if you have one child being cared for	70% of up to £135 per week
Childcare Tax Credit - if you have two or more children being cared for	70% of up to £200 per week altogether
Per additional partner in a polygamous marriage	£27.20

- You must have at least one child for whom you are responsible who is normally living with you. This usually means that you or your partner are eligible for Child Benefit for the child. The child must be aged under 16, or under 19, if he is still in full-time education.

- You must have capital of not more than £8,000. Capital means any lump sum or one-off payment, savings, property, redundancy payments, etc. If the value of this is over £8,000, it may be worth taking advice because some capital can be ignored so you could still qualify. The value of your home is ignored if you live in it.

- You must have income below a certain amount. Some of your income is ignored or partially ignored. For example, your pay is considered nett of tax and National Insurance, certain other expenses and 50 per cent of contributions towards a pension scheme. Income such as interest on savings under £3,000, Child Benefit, Child Maintenance and Disability Living Allowance are ignored. Take advice. Also, there are special rules on other kinds of income. See *Income Support* and *Job Seeker's Allowance: Income Based*, as the rules are the same.

NB If the above applies and you are disabled, you do qualify but you may be better off claiming Disabled Person's Tax Credit instead.

A note on Childcare Tax Credit

The qualifications for this credit:

- You have to have at least one child who you are paying to be looked after by a registered childminder, or another registered childcare provider such as a nursery, after school club, breakfast club or other day care service. If the person looking after your child is a friend or relative that's OK, so long as you're paying him and he is registered. Note that while you are on maternity leave, you cannot include childcare for a new baby, and you can only include other children if you already had some childcare costs to pay before the new baby was born.

- You have to be a lone parent, or, if you have a partner, you and your partner must be working 16+ hours per week. Alternatively, you will still qualify if you have a partner and one of you is working and the other is disabled or suffers ill-health.

You may find that your childcare costs fluctuate, for example, between term-times and holidays. In this case, special rules are applied to arrive at an average cost for the purposes of working out your entitlement.

Note the maximums in the Amount box. For example, if you have two children being cared for, and you have to pay £250 per week, the credit in your case will be £175 (70 per cent of £250).

Making a claim

Obtain form WFTC 1, available from the Tax Credit office (see *Useful addresses*), Inland Revenue Enquiry Offices or your local social security office. The form will tell you which information and documents you will need to enclose - such as payslips (or the TC500 form mentioned above), a profit and loss account or a statement of earnings and expenses if you are self-employed, and details from whoever provides your childcare. If you haven't got all the information to hand, send the application in anyway as you can always send in the necessary documents later.

However, if you have just started work after being unemployed, the local Jobcentre may be able to help speed up your claim as they have a special arrangement with the Tax Credit Office. The Office will calculate your entitlement based on your average income. This will be based on the six weeks prior to the date you claim if you are paid weekly or the three months prior if you are paid monthly. If you've just started working, don't let that delay your claim. If you haven't worked for nine weeks, you can ask your employer to complete a form (TC500) that comes with the WFTC Claim Pack and on this your employer can confirm your hours and earnings.

Note that if you have a new baby, or adopt a child, you can choose to cancel your claim and apply again. If you do this within a month of telling the Tax Credit Office, your benefit should not be interrupted. If you are receiving WFTC already and your claim is due to expire before April 2003, you will need to send in a renewal claim to take you until that date.

Payment

From autumn 2002, the Tax Credit Office will pay you directly. Alternatively, you can arrange for your partner to be paid directly if you wish.

Your payments will run until 7 April 2003, but you are still obliged to report to the Tax Credit Office any change of circumstances, such as revised childcare costs or changed income. However, most changes in circumstances will not affect what you receive, although as ever there are a few exceptions. For example, if one of the children you are claiming for leaves home and then claims Income Support or Income Based Job Seeker's Allowance (or someone includes him in his claim), or he reaches 16 or leaves full-time education.

Getting further information

Phone the WFTC helpline at the Tax Credit Office (see *Useful addresses*) for information and a quick calculation of your entitlement. This information will not be final, because the real decision cannot be made until they have processed your application, but it gives you a good idea of your position. The Inland Revenue website allows you to do an online calculation of your entitlement.

Working Tax Credit (WTC)

Are you bringing up a family and finding your finances are stretched? This benefit may help to top up your earnings and help with childcare expenses. It is a new benefit starting in April 2003 replacing the Working Families' Tax Credit (WFTC). At the time of writing this book, not all information on this benefit has been published, so if you have other queries, take advice.

Qualification checklist

The following must apply to you, but if you are claiming as a couple, it must apply to both of you:

- You are aged 16 or over.
- You are either working as employed or self-employed, or you expect to be starting work within the next seven days, and the work is expected to last four or more weeks.
- Your work is for 30 hours or more per week. You still qualify if you are receiving Statutory Maternity Pay (SMP) or Maternity Allowance, or Statutory Sick Pay (SSP) provided that you were working 30 hours before you claimed these benefits. If you are off sick whilst self-employed you qualify if the 30 hours applied before you went off sick.
- Alternatively, you can still qualify if your work is for at least 16 hours per week, but only if you, or your partner if any, have responsibility for bringing up a child. The above exceptions for maternity and sickness apply.
- You can also qualify if you work at least 16 hours a week and you have a physical or mental disability that prevents you from working more hours. Again, the exceptions for maternity and sickness apply.

- Your income is below a certain amount (see *Amount box*), although your capital (that is any lump sum or one off payment, savings or property) will have no effect on the Tax Credit.

How to claim

If you are receiving Working Families' Tax Credit or Disabled Person's Tax Credit, you should receive a letter from the Inland Revenue inviting you to claim in time to be paid from 7 April 2003. Otherwise, you can obtain a claim form from an Inland Revenue Enquiry Centre or Jobcentre. Alternatively, log on to the Inland Revenue website and you can claim online. If you are a couple, you have to claim jointly. You will need to provide details of your present circumstances, and details of your income over the previous tax year, and you will be asked to estimate your income over the current tax year. Of course, the more you are through the tax year when you actually claim, the better your estimate will be! You will also have to provide evidence of your situation e.g. childcare, any disability and employment.

If the variation between these two sets of figures is less than a prescribed amount, the previous year's income will be used to work out your entitlement. However, if the variation is greater than this amount, your entitlement will be worked out from the current year. So, for example, if you are claiming in January 2003, and your income over the previous tax year (from April 2001 to March 2002) was £10,000, and your estimated income over the current tax year (April 2002 to March 2003) is £13,000, the Inland Revenue will usually work out your entitlement by looking at the current year.

Before the end of the tax year in which you are receiving WTC, the Inland Revenue will ask you for evidence of your actual income for the previous year. If these figures prove that you overestimated your income, you will probably be asked to repay some of the benefit (or the overpayment may be deducted from your entitlement or, if you are an employee, collected by increasing the amount of tax you have to pay through the PAYE system. On the other hand, if you underestimated your income, you should be paid extra WTC to make up the difference!

Payment

If you are claiming as a couple you can decide which of you should receive the payment. If you are in work, you will usually be paid via your employer with your wages, although you will be paid directly, for example, if you are on maternity leave when you apply or if you are self-employed.

Amount box

The basic maximum allowance is £29.32 per week, but there are additional maximum amounts you may get, depending on your circumstances, if you meet any of the following criteria:

- You or your partner (if any) has a disability. If you have a partner and you both have a disability, each of you will receive a separate addition for this. See *Disabled Person's Tax Credit* because if you qualify as disabled for this benefit, you should also qualify for this element of WTC - £30.20, and an extra £16.63 if you have a severe disability.
- You work at least 30 hours per week (or, if you have a partner, you do these hours between you) - £11.92.
- You have a second adult living with you. You will not qualify for this if neither of you work 30 hours or more and one of you is aged 50 or over - £28.84.
- You are a single parent - £28.84.
- You or your partner is aged 50 or over. If you have a partner and you are both aged 50 or over, each of you will receive a separate addition for this - £20.09, or £30.09 if you are working 30+ hours.
- If you have to pay to have your child looked after whilst you are working. This is similar to the childcare credit that forms part of Working Families' Tax Credit so see the chapter on this benefit.- up to 70% of your childcare costs, up to £135 maximum for one child, £200 for two or more children.

To work out your actual entitlement add up the maximum you could get, then deduct from this your income. At least the first £5,060 of annual income is ignored, but more than this could also be ignored depending on the source of the income and your circumstances - take advice.

If you claim in advance of a tax year, i.e. before 6 April each year, you will be paid the same amount for the whole of the tax year. If you claim during the tax year in which you want to be paid, your claim will start from the date it is made and will be paid until the end of the tax year.

Once you have claimed, you may not have to reclaim each year to receive WTC. You will just need to declare your circumstances on your self-assessment tax return. However, if any changes in circumstances happen to you during the tax year, you should report them as this could lead to you getting more WTC, or less, or losing entitlement altogether! If you are single and you live with a partner or are getting married, your claim will be stopped and you will have to make a fresh (joint) claim. The same will happen if you split up with your partner.

Appendix

Income Support, Job Seeker's Allowance: Income Based, Minimum Income Guarantee and Disability Income Guarantee - the basics

Use this chapter if you are interested in Income Based Job Seeker's Allowance, Minimum Income Guarantee, Disability Income Guarantee and Income Support for people in different circumstances. These benefits have certain rules in common. If the conditions below apply to you, you are on the road to qualifying so read these first and then go back to the chapter you think might apply to you.

Qualification checklist

You may qualify if the following applies to you:

- If you are claiming Income Support, you qualify if you are aged between 16 and 60 but if you are over 60, you can claim the Minimum Income Guarantee which is Income Support under another name.
- If you are claiming Income Based Job Seeker's Allowance, you have to be aged 16-60.
- If you are working, this must be for less than 16 hours (if you have a partner in work you can still qualify so long as he is working less than 24 hours). If your hours, or your partner's hours, fluctuate then it's your weekly average that must be below these limits. However, if your partner works more than 16 hours, you may be better off claiming Working Families' Tax Credit or Working Tax Credit. Having said this, there are a few situations where you can be working more than 16 hours and still qualify, for example, if you are a childminder working at home so take advice.
- If you or your partner normally work more than this but are off sick or on maternity leave, you can still qualify.
- You are not getting Contribution Based Job Seeker's Allowance.
- You or your partner cannot receive Income Based Job Seeker's Allowance and Income Support at the same time.
- Your or your partner's income must be below a certain amount. Some of your income is ignored or partially ignored so take advice.

- For example, your pay is considered nett of tax and National Insurance, plus certain other expenses and 50 per cent of contributions towards a pension scheme. Then a further £5 per week is ignored (£10 if you are a couple, £20 if you are a single parent, or you or your partner are a carer or disabled). Disability Living Allowance or Attendance Allowance are ignored. Take advice.
- If you let out part of the home you live in, the first £4 per week you charge for each tenant (or the first £9.40 if you also charge for heating) is ignored. If you have a boarder on a commercial basis in your own home (that is you provide food, cleaning, etc) you can ignore the first £20 per week and then half of any balance remaining.
- What about interest on savings? The actual interest you receive is ignored and instead you are treated as having extra income of £1 for each £250 (or part of £250) of capital above £3,000. For example, if you have £5,114, you will be deemed to have income of £5 per week (that's 2,114 excess which is four lots of £250 = £4 and one part of £250 = £1).
- If your capital is over £8,000, you do not qualify at all. Capital means any lump sum or one-off payment, savings, property, redundancy payments, etc. If the value of your capital is over £8,000 (£12,000 in the case of Minimum Income Guarantee), it may be worth taking advice because some capital can be ignored so you could still qualify. Note that the value of your home is ignored if you live in it.
- If you are living with a partner, his capital and income is combined with yours in working out your entitlement.

How to work out your entitlement

To work out how much you may be entitled, follow these two steps. These can also be used to work out your Housing Benefit or Council Tax Benefit.

Step 1 Make a total of all the elements in the Amount box below that might apply to you. These elements make up what is called your 'applicable amount'. You can include your mortgage or other housing costs (ignore these costs if you are claiming Housing Benefit or Council Tax Benefit).

Step 2 Now subtract any weekly income (or what counts as your income) from the total figure you have arrived at from Step 1.

Whatever is left is your entitlement. If there is nothing left, or if your income is in fact greater than your applicable amount, then you do not qualify.

Amount box

Element	Circumstances	Amount
Personal Allowances		
If you are single (no children)	Age 16 or 17 *This may be increased to a higher rate of £42.70, for example, if you qualify for a disability premium (see below) or because you have to live away from your parents because your relationship with them has broken down.*	£32.50
	Age 18-24	£42.70
	Age 25 or over	£53.95
If you are a single parent	Aged 16 or 17 *Again, this may be increased to the higher rate of £42.70 in certain circumstances as above.*	£32.50
	Aged 18 or over	£53.95
If you live with a spouse or partner	Both of you aged 18 or over	£84.65
	Both aged 16 or 17 and at least one of you is responsible for a child	£64.45
	Both of you 16 or 17 if one or other of you qualify	£32.50
	Both of you 16 or 17 if you both qualify	£64.45
	Both of you 16 or 17 if one of you qualify but at the higher rate for 16/17 year-olds	£42.70
	One aged over 18 and the other 16 or 17 if the under 18 year-old would have qualified if claiming on his own	£84.65
	One aged over 25 and the other 16 or 17 if the younger person is not entitled in his own right	**£53.95**
	One aged over 18 and the other 16 or 17 if the younger person is not entitled in his own right	**£42.70**
	Polygamous marriage - for each spouse living in the same household	£30.70
Amounts for your children	For each child under 16	£33.50
	For each child aged 16-18	£34.50

ELEMENT	CIRCUMSTANCES	AMOUNT
Special Allowances called 'premiums'	Family premium *Paid, as you look after a child under 16, or a young person under 19 and in full-time education*	£14.75
	Disabled child premium - per child *You are eligible if you have a child who is blind or for whom you get Disability Living Allowance*	£35.50
	Pensioner premium - if you are single	£44.20
	Pensioner premium - if you are claiming as a couple *A pensioner premium is paid if you or your partner are aged 60 or over*	£65.15
	Disability premium - if you are a single parent	£23.00
	Disability premium - if you are claiming as a couple *A disability premium is paid if you or your partner is under 60 and disabled, i.e. if registered blind or receiving benefits for sickness or disability, or Disabled Person's Tax Credit, or if the Social Security office considers you are incapable of work. This premium cannot be paid at the same time as any of the pensioner premiums*	£32.80
	Enhanced disability premium - if you qualify yourself and you are a single person	£11.25
	Enhanced disability premium - if you live as a couple and at least one of you qualifies	£16.25
	Enhanced disability premium - for each child who qualifies *This premium is paid if you or your partner, or a child you look after is entitled to the highest rate care component of Disability Living Allowance and is under 60. The adult rates can be paid in addition to any other premium except the pensioner premiums. The child rate can be paid in addition to any other premium so long as he doesn't have over £3,000 in capital*	£11.25
	Severe disability premium - either if you are single and qualify, or if you are a couple and one of you qualifies	£42.25

Element	Circumstances	Amount
	Severe disability premium - if you live as a couple and you both qualify *If you are getting Attendance Allowance or the higher or middle rate care component of Disability Living Allowance.* *NB You will only qualify for this if you've got someone living with you such as a grown-up son or daughter or parents, and no-one gets Invalid Care Allowance for looking after you. Entitlement to this premium is not affected by any other premiums you may qualify for*	£84.50
	Carer's premium - if you are single or a couple and one of you qualifies	£24.80
	Carer's premium - if you live as a couple and you both qualify *If you or your partner is entitled to and receiving Invalid Care Allowance. This applies even if you are entitled to Invalid Care Allowance but receiving another benefit instead. Entitlement continues until eight weeks after entitlement to Invalid Care Allowance stops. If both members of a couple are entitled to Invalid Care Allowance, you are entitled to two carer's premiums*	£49.60
	Bereavement premium *If you were 55-60 on 9 April 2001, and you were getting Bereavement Allowance following the death of your husband or wife on or after that date, and, within eight weeks of ceasing Bereavement Allowance, you're getting Income Support, Housing Benefit or Council Tax Benefit*	£21.55
Housing costs	If you are claiming Income Support or Income Based Job Seeker's Allowance, you can also add in your weekly repayments on your mortgage and some loans	See *Mortgage and other loans - help with repayments*
	If you are a crown tenant, or if you pay ground rent as a leaseholder. Some service charges can also be included. Take advice	Your rents (other rents may be covered by Housing Benefit)

Tax allowances and tax reliefs and your Tax Return - some general points

Tax allowances

What they are

The Government sets tax rates each year, which means you have to pay a percentage of your income to the Inland Revenue. The tax allowances (set out in previous chapters) are basically annual amounts relating to personal circumstances which can be deducted from your income to ensure that some of it is tax free. For example, disregarding National Insurance, if you have tax allowances totalling £4,615 and you earn £12,000, you pay no tax on that £4,615 which leaves £7,385 to pay tax on.

If you happen to earn less than your tax allowances in a tax year, but you still paid tax, you may be entitled to a tax rebate. If in the above example you only earn £4,000 in a year and you paid tax, as you earnings were less than your allowances you will be able to claim all this tax back as a rebate.

How to claim

Except for the Personal Allowance which you should get automatically, you have to claim tax allowances by completing a Tax Return. You receive the allowances in the form of less tax to pay.

How you receive them

You don't actually receive them but it is an amount you can deduct from your income to reduce the amount of Income Tax you have to pay, or, if you are an employee, it is deducted by them under the PAYE system and apportioned equally throughout the year. For example, if you are paid monthly, you will be paid one twelfth of the allowance each month.

Tax reliefs

What they are

The Government decides that you should not have to pay tax on certain items and as a result, gives you tax relief. So, unlike tax allowances, tax reliefs are not amounts fixed in advance, as they may be all or part of your actual spending, or in some cases your estimated spending. Therefore, if in the above example you also qualify for tax relief on expenditure of say £339, that will be another £339 of your income that is tax free, so you now only have to pay tax £7,046 (£7,385 - £339).

How to claim

Tax relief is mostly claimed by completing a Tax Return, although in some cases if you are paying tax under the Pay as You Earn system (PAYE) you can claim via your employer. Details appear on each in the various chapters on types of relief.

How you receive them

If you qualify for tax relief in connection with your employment, the Inland Revenue will ask your employer to allow to that amount tax-free as for allowances. Other tax relief, if it has to be claimed in the Tax Return, will be allowed as tax-free income so you will have less tax to pay.

The Tax Return - some general points

Tax allowances and some tax reliefs can be claimed all at once, on the 10-page booklet called the Tax Return. Note that the sending in of a Tax Return is compulsory if you have been asked to do so by the Inland Revenue, or if you have received any income or capital gains during the previous tax year not previously declared.

In the Tax Return you declare your circumstances, your income and expenditure for the previous tax year and claim appropriate tax reliefs and allowances as set out in earlier chapters. As well as the Tax Return, there are up to nine sets of supplementary pages for particular types of income. These cover self-employment, employment, share schemes, partnerships, land and property, trusts, share schemes, foreign income, capital gains and non-residence in the country. Although you must complete the Tax Return booklet, you won't need to fill in all the supplementary pages, only those that relate to your circumstances, for example, if you are an employee, or self-employed, or if you have shares.

The Tax Return booklet and the supplementary pages you need may be sent to you automatically by the Inland Revenue, but if not, you can obtain them either from the Inland Revenue's Orderline, your nearest Taxpayer Enquiry Service, the Inland Revenue office that deals with your tax (the Taxpayer Enquiry Service or your employer, if you have one, can advise you where this is), or from the Inland Revenue website at www.inlandrevenue.gov.uk/sa.

If your financial affairs are complicated you may have to instruct an accountant, or other tax adviser.

If you are filling in the forms yourself, for help you can use the Tax Return Guide and supplementary guides that come with the forms, or buy one of the tax guides published each year following the Budget. For basic queries, you can visit your local Taxpayer Enquiry Centre, or use the Inland Revenue telephone helpline.

Calculating your tax liability

If you send in the Tax Return by 30 September, the Inland Revenue staff will definitely work out how much tax, if any, you have to pay after tax allowances and tax reliefs. If you leave it beyond that date, this may still be done depending on staff workload, but the chances are you'll have to do all the calculations yourself. This may be pretty straightforward if most of your income is from earnings as an employee, as you will have paid tax under the PAYE scheme anyway.

However, things can get more complicated if you have self-employed or other income, particularly if you want to claim as many tax reliefs as possible. In that case, you will need to use the Tax Calculation Guide or, in some cases, the Comprehensive Tax Calculation Guide, available from the Inland Revenue Orderline or website as above. Alternatively, you can use the electronic tax return - see below.

Sending in your Tax Return

Take or post your completed forms to the Inland Revenue office which deals with your tax, or to your local Taxpayer Enquiry Centre. The forms will tell you to enclose certain documents relevant to your circumstances, for example, a P60 if you were employed during the tax year (a statement of your income from employment, and tax paid on it) or bank statements and records of income and expenditure in some cases.

The internet option

You can, if you wish, fill in your forms electronically. Most of them are now available online. They have built in software to calculate your tax for you, although in some cases you may be referred to commercially available software. For further information contact the Taxpayer Enquiry Centre or look at www.inlandrevenue.gov.uk or www.gateway.gov.uk. Do register directly if you are comfortable with the internet. You will be sent an ID and password by post or you can use a digital certificate. Once you've completed the forms, you can either send them via the internet or print off a paper version to deal with as above.

The deadline

The final deadline for getting your Tax Return in for the previous tax year is 31 January of the following year, so for a 2002/03 tax return the deadline would be 31 January 2004. If you haven't got all the details of your income or expenditure, you can estimate this and send in final figures later as you will be expected to do this as soon as possible.

If you fail to get your Tax Return in by this deadline, you can be charged a penalty of £100 (or the equivalent of the tax due if that is less than £100). Also, the Inland Revenue will issue what's called a determination. This is an estimate of how much tax you should pay. The only way you can then get to pay less tax would be to complete the tax return and tax calculation with all the evidence showing that the estimate was wrong! The more you delay sending in the Tax Return the more penalties you could end up having to pay. If you send in your Tax Return and then discover you've made a mistake, for example, you have failed to declare certain income, or failed to claim a tax relief, you have up to 12 months from sending the Return in to ask to amend your Return. If the Inland Revenue themselves discover any obvious errors, they can amend your Return but must do so within nine months of receiving it.

Inland Revenue checking up on you

How do the Inland Revenue keep a check on things? Your Tax Return may be selected at random for an enquiry, or more likely it will be selected if they think something isn't quite right, either in what you have or haven't declared, or the way you've calculated your tax liability including tax reliefs and allowances. You will be advised whether the enquiry is into your whole Return, or some part of it - say a particular relief you are claiming. Once the enquiry is complete, the tax office will notify you of their findings. They may also order you to pay more tax, for example, because they think you should not qualify for a certain tax relief or allowance. If you disagree with their findings, you can appeal.

In brief...

You might also qualify for financial help in the following ways:

Getting paid to stay on at school

If you are staying on at school or going to college you may qualify for a weekly payment of *Educational Maintenance Allowance*, but at present this is only possible if you live in certain pilot areas. Payments are between £30 and £40 per week.

Contact the Connexions Service or Local Education Authority to see if you are in a pilot area. If you are, they will tell you how to claim.

Grants to help with your employment costs if you are disabled

You can apply for practical help and grants under the *Access to Work* scheme to help you overcome work related obstacles arising from your disability. The support is tailor-made to your individual needs in your job, if you are employed or self-employed. This can include making adaptations in the workplace, paying for a support worker and expenses for travelling to work. You can also arrange to be paid to attend work preparation courses. If you do this, you can stay on the benefits you are getting or claim an employment rehabilitation allowance and other expenses instead. Take advice. Support including any payments last for a maximum of three years.

Payments may be paid to you or your employer if you have one, depending on what they are for.

Contact your local Jobcentre for an application form and further details.

Grant on starting a new job

You can claim a grant of £100 if you are starting a new job of 16 hours or more - including a job under the New Deal scheme. The job must be expected to last more than five weeks. You must be 25 or over, and receiving Income Support, Job Seeker's Allowance, Incapacity Benefit, or Severe Disablement Allowance for the past 12 months. You won't qualify if you are also entitled to Lone Parent Run On.

Claim from your local Jobcentre within three weeks of starting the job.

Getting paid to receive training

There are a variety of government training schemes, some compulsory if you have been unemployed for a period, some voluntary.

If you are 16-18 and unemployed, you can receive £40 per week under the *Work Based Training for Young People* scheme. If you are 25 or over, you can receive your existing benefits plus £10 a week under the *Work Based Learning for Adults* scheme (*this is called 'Training for Work' in Scotland*).

Under the *New Deal for 18-24 year-olds* you could be offered up to six months' work with a voluntary organisation or an environmental project with benefits including a Training Allowance, a £400 top-up payment paid in weekly or fortnightly instalments, and travel costs over £4 a week. Alternatively, you could choose to undertake a one-year training course with work experience. The Training Allowance will be the same amount as you normally get in benefits but with travel expenses and, in some cases, childcare and other course expenses.

Under the *New Deal for people aged 25 plus*, there is an intensive period of 13-26 weeks when you have to undergo intensive job search or training. You will receive a Training Allowance at the same level as your normal benefits plus an extra £15.38 per week.

There are also voluntary New Deal schemes for other groups. They too can pay Training Allowances and other incentives to help you back into work. These are:

New Deal for partners
New Deal for lone parents
New Deal for disabled people
New Deal for over 50s

Contact your Jobcentre for details.

Payment to take on a job on a trial basis

If you are 25 or over, have been unemployed for at least six months and you take up a paid job for up to 15 days, you can continue to receive your normal benefits and claim travel expenses of up to £10 per day and also meal costs of up to £1.50 per day. Your benefits are not affected if you do not continue with the job.

Claim from your local Jobcentre.

Travel expenses paid to go to a job interview

If you or your partner are unemployed and receiving Job Seeker's Allowance or National Insurance Credits, you can claim for your travel costs to a job interview beyond your normal travelling distance, if the job is 30 or more hours per week.

Claim form from your local Jobcentre.

Paying less Council Tax if you are disabled

You can get a reduction in your Council Tax if you or someone else resident in your home is disabled, and you have in your home a second bathroom or kitchen for his use, or another room needed by that person, or you have enough space in the home for that person to use his wheelchair indoors.

Apply to the local council. Your Council Tax liability will be reduced to the amount payable on the valuation band immediately below that of your home, so if your home is in Band D you will be billed at Band C instead.

Payment if vaccine caused you to be disabled

A *Vaccine Damage Payment* can be claimed if you are assessed at 60 per cent or more disabled as a result of you being vaccinated against a specific disease, or your mother being vaccinated whilst pregnant with you. Claim any time up to the age of 21, but your parents have to claim for you if you are under 18. You may also claim on behalf of someone who died as a result of the vaccination, or if you contracted polio from another person who was vaccinated against it. The payment is a lump sum or £100,000.

The rules have been changed recently so if you were turned down before it is worth claiming again. Contact the *Vaccine Damage Payments Unit*. See *Useful addresses*.

Grants for insulation against traffic or rail noise

If you are suffering noise because a new road or railway line has been built to pass near your home, you may be able to claim to have your home insulated.

Contact *The Highways Agency (England)* or the *Scottish Office Development Department* or the *National Assembly for Wales Highways Directorate* (see *Useful addresses*).

For rail routes, contact the *Department of the Environment, Transport and the Regions.*

Payment if you are victim of a crime

You can claim from the *Criminal Injuries Compensation Scheme* if you suffer a personal injury as a result of a crime of violence in the UK. This may include psychological trauma as well as physical injury and includes child abuse and pregnancy and sexually transmitted diseases contracted as a result of rape. Domestic violence may also be included.

Get further information and a claim form from the *Criminal Injuries Compensation Authority* (see *Useful addresses).*

Payment if you are injured by an uninsured or identified driver

If you suffered a personal injury caused by a motor cyclist or motorist who was uninsured or unidentified, you may be able to claim for damages from the *Motor Insurers' Bureau.*

For further information contact the *Motor Insurers' Bureau (MIB)* - see *Useful addresses).*

Help with car hire, purchase or adaptation

The *Motability* scheme allows you to either hire, or buy on hire purchase, a car or electric wheelchair. You can also get help with adaptations to your car, and in some cases, money towards the cost of driving lessons. You have to receive the higher rate mobility component of Disability Living Allowance or War Pensioner's Mobility Supplement as part of your War Disablement Pension.

For further information contact *Motability.*

Getting exemption from road tax

You can claim exemption from road tax if you are receiving the higher rate mobility component of Disability Living Allowance, or Mobility Supplement as part of your War Disablement Pension. Use your vehicle excise duty exemption form to apply for a 'tax exempt disc' from the Vehicle Licensing Agency.

You should automatically be sent an exemption form when you receive the benefit, but if not, contact the body that deals with your benefit (see *Disability Living Allowance* or *War Disablement Pension*).

Help with the cost of using a solicitor

Under the Community Legal Service (CLS) Legal Help scheme you may qualify for free legal advice or assistance with your case, but only if the solicitor you use is part of the scheme. It is always worth considering as many people can qualify. Your income or capital must be below a set limit depending on your circumstances. Note that if you receive Income Support or Income Based Job Seeker's Allowance you will automatically qualify if your capital is below the set limit. Be warned, not all legal subject areas are covered. The solicitor may be subject to a time limit on the work, and if you are successful in achieving compensation as a result of using the solicitor under this scheme, you may have to pay certain costs out of your winnings.

Find out from local advice services which solicitors operate under the scheme in your area for the subject you want help with. Alternatively, consult the CLS directory in the local library or use their website at www.justask.org.uk. You can also find out by phoning the national office of the Law Society or enquire at any solicitor office which displays the CLS logo. In Scotland the scheme is slightly different so contact the Legal Aid Board (see *Useful addresses*).

Travelling expenses on release from prison

You can claim reasonable travel expenses, say to go home, when you are released from prison permanently or temporarily.

Apply at the prison.

Help with travel expenses to visit someone in prison

You can apply for payments to meet travel costs, and the cost of an overnight stay, to visit a close relative or partner in prison if you are getting Income Support, Income Based Job Seeker's Allowance, the various tax credits or if you are not on these benefits but on a low income.

Get an application form from the social security office or the *Assisted Prison Visits Unit* (see *Useful addresses*).

Help with travel expenses to hospital

You can qualify for help with travel expenses to and from hospital if you are getting Income Support, Income Based Job Seeker's Allowance, Working Families' Tax Credit or Disabled Person's Tax Credit or if you are not on these benefits but on a low income (see *Health Service charges - help under the Low Income Scheme*). You can also claim for another person to travel with you if you are not capable of getting there on your own, or you can claim if you are taking your child for treatment.

The hospital will refund your charges if you produce proof of entitlement. If you haven't yet claimed under the Low Income Scheme, ask the hospital for form HC5 so you can claim for a refund if you qualify. The hospital has to fill in part of it.

An allowance if you are between jobs or training places

You can claim an allowance of £15 a week or £3 a day for up to eight weeks (40 days) in a 52 week period if you are under 18 and you have left a job or training place and you are registered for work or training. No one must be claiming Child Benefit for you. If this is the only income you receive, you will be able to claim maximum Housing Benefit and Council Tax Benefit as if you were receiving Income Support (see *Income Support if you are a young person on a training course*).

Claim from the Careers Office or Jobcentre where you registered for training.

Help to meet the cost of a sight test and glasses from your employer

If you spend a lot of your working day using a computer, your employer should reimburse you the cost of a sight test every two years and pay for glasses where these are needed to help you with your work.

Apply to your employer.

Payments while you are laid off from your job

If your employer has less work for you, you may be laid off (i.e. asked not to come into work for a temporary period) or put on short time working (asked to work for less hours per week). For every full day this happens, you may be entitled to claim a Guarantee Payment but only if you are not paid your wages or salary. The maximum rate per day is £17, and you can only receive a payment for a maximum of five days in any three month period. Apply to your employer.

Help with your TV Licence fee

You do not have to pay for a TV licence for your main home if you are 75 or over. Apply when you are 75 and then you will receive a new one automatically each year. If you live in a care home or certain local council or housing association's sheltered housing, you only have to pay £5. If you are registered blind you can get a licence for half price; just take your registration document to the post office when you renew your licence. You can get TV sound only receivers and you do not need a licence for these.

For a care home or sheltered housing, the home manager or warden should apply for you. For a TV sound only receiver, contact Portset (see *Useful addresses*).

Help with meeting your charges for community care

If you are receiving care arranged by your local council Social Services Department, you may be charged a weekly amount depending on your income. If you cannot afford the charges, ask for them to be reduced or waived. This is a matter for the discretion of the council.

Contact your local Social Services Department.

An allowance where you do not satisfy the normal benefit rules

This is a special allowance called an *urgent cases payment*, that may be paid to you if you don't otherwise qualify for benefit as you are subject to immigration control, or you are treated as having income but it hasn't actually been paid to you.

In order to claim, you have to convince the Social Security office that you or your family will suffer hardship if you are not paid.

If you face financial hardship while studying

Each college and university has *Access Funds* which you can apply for if you are a student in hardship. The qualifying rules and the amounts you can receive will depend on the college's policy. Take advice.

Apply to the relevant department of your college or university. The Students Union may help.

Free school meals

If you or your child (under 16) arranges to have school meals, you can ask to be exempt from the charge if you or your partner is receiving Income Based Job Seeker's Allowance or Income Support. The school may allow you to be exempt in other circumstances.

Enquire at the school.

Paying for your children's school meals if you are a student

If you are a student with dependant children aged 3-16, you can apply to their Local Education Authority (LEA) for a means-tested grant to pay for your children's school meals.

Get a claim form from the LEA.

Travel concessions

There may be local schemes in your area that allow travel in certain circumstances on public transport at a cheaper rate, for example, if you are blind or otherwise disabled, over pension age, or under 16. You can also buy nationally available railcards which permit discounted rail travel at certain times with certain types of ticket e.g. for people with children, for students, for disabled people, and for people aged 60 or over.

For local schemes, contact the local council or local transport operator.

For rail travel, contact the train operator.

Grants from trusts

There are many possible sources of grants (and sometimes allowances) paid by trusts. Mostly they have been set up to help people in certain categories, and each will have their own qualifying rules. Take advice, or go to your local library and consult the reference section

By way of example, the Prince's Trust provides financial help to young people under 25 to help them start up as self-employed, the Macfarlane Trust assists people with haemophilia, and the Family Fund Trust provides grants and information to families caring for a severely disabled child. Write to them for an application form.

Useful guides to trusts are published by the Directory of Social Change.

Taking out a loan to cover expenses

This book sets out the main grants and allowances available. Loans don't fall into this category so they have not been included, but statutory loans are available to help you meet daily living expenses. Take advice. For example, if you are a student, you can apply for a student loan, and if you receive Income Support, Income Based Job Seeker's Allowance, you can apply for a *crisis loan* for emergencies or a *budgeting loan* for other lump sum expenditure.

For student loans, contact your local education authority or, in Scotland, the Students Award Agency for Scotland (SAAS) - see *Useful addresses*.

For crisis and budgeting loans, apply to your local social security office.

If your employer goes bust

To claim wages including overtime, commission and holiday pay ask for Form RP1 from your employer's representative (e.g. receiver or liquidator) if one has been appointed. To claim for compensation for not getting notice ask for form RP2. Send these to the Redundancy Payment Office - see *Redundancy Payments Scheme*. If your employer has not appointed a representative claim direct from them, failing that to claim via an Employment Tribunal or apply to have the employer's business wound up - but take advice first.

You are self-employed and you want to avoid paying National Insurance contributions

If you can show that your nett earnings from self-employment for the tax year are expected to be low (currently less than £4,025), you can apply to be exempted from having to pay National Insurance contributions.

Get a form from your local Inland Revenue Enquiry Office or from the Inland Revenue Contributions Office (see *Useful addresses*).

Grants for students

If you are a student, you may qualify for certain grants. For example, if you have dependant(s), you may be eligible for a grant to cover childcare expenses, school meals for your child, travel costs, books and equipment, and your extra costs if you have to run two homes as a result of living away. There is another grant available to meet certain travel expenses. Take advice.

The grants are managed by your Local Education Authority (LEA) or in Scotland, the Student Awards Agency for Scotland (SAAS). Ask them for details of their claims procedures and priorities for help.

The SAAS or the Department for Education and Skills (DfES) information line can provide further advice, as can the National Union of Students (see *Useful addresses*).

Students - help with tuition fees

If you are, or are about to become, a full-time student in England, Wales or Northern Ireland, you and your parents may qualify for help with tuition fees. This will depend on your and your family's income. The most you will have to pay is £1,100. If your parents' residual income is less than £20,480, you will pay nothing. If their income is above £30,502, you will have to pay the full £1,100.

Claim from your LEA at the same time as when you claim your student loan. They will assess how much, if anything, you will have to pay.

You want to avoid paying tax on your savings

If you expect that your taxable income will be less than your tax allowances, you can arrange for your bank or building society to pay your interest without any tax taken off. Ask them for a registration form or pick up form R85 from your local Inland Revenue Enquiry Office.

If you are disabled and you are a full-time or part-time student (or you want to be one!)

You may qualify for an allowance to cover the extra costs of studying with a disability. The grants are managed by your Local Education Authority (LEA) or in Scotland, the Student Awards Agency for Scotland (SAAS) - see *Useful addresses*. Ask them for details of their claims procedures and claim for all of the extra expenses that arise because of your disability. They will consider which of the expenses to meet, up to certain maximums, depending on their policies and priorities. The kinds of things you may get help with could be a computer, recording equipment, other special equipment and aids, extra heating and dietary needs, help with readers and note takers, and other paid helpers.

Paying less Council Tax if you live alone

If you live alone, you may be entitled to have your Council tax bill reduced by 25 per cent. Apply to your local council.

Useful addresses

Assisted Prison Visits Unit
PO Box 2512
Birmingham B15 1SD

Tel: 0121 626 2797

Benefits Enquiry Line
Tel: 0800 882 200 (0800 220 674 in Northern Ireland)
Minicom: 0800 243 355
Website: www.dwp.gov.uk
Website: www.ssani.gov.uk (in Northern Ireland)

Child Benefit Centre
DWP (Washington)
PO Box 1
Newcastle upon Tyne NE88 1AA

Tel: 0870 155 5540
Email: Child-Benefit@dwp.gsi.gov.uk
Website: www.dwp.gov.uk

Children's Tax Credit Helpline
Tel: 0845 300 1036

Criminal Injuries Compensation Authority
Tay House
300 Bath Street
Glasgow G2 4LN

Tel: 0800 358 3601

Department for Education and Skills (DfES)
Information Lines: 0800 731 9133/0800 210 280

Department for Work and Pensions
Pensions Direct
Tyneview Park
Whitley Road
Benton
Newcastle Upon Tyne NE 98 1BA

Tel: 0191 203 0203

Department of the Environment, Transport and the Regions
Eland House
Bressenden Place
London SW1E 5DU

Tel: 020 7276 3000

Directory of Social Change
London Office
24 Stephenson Way
London NW1 2DP

Tel: 020 7209 5151
Fax: 020 7391 4804
Email: books@dsc.org.uk

Disability Benefits Unit
Government Buildings
Warbreck House
Warbreck Hill
Blackpool FY2 0YJ

Tel: 0845 712 3456

The Family Fund Trust
PO Box 50
York YO1 9ZK

Tel: 01904 621 115
Fax: 01904 652 625
Textphone: 01904 658 085
Email: info@familyfundtrust.org.uk Website: www.familyfundtrust.org.uk

Federation of Independent Advice Centres
4 Dean's Court
St Pauls Churchyard
London EC4V 5AA

Tel: 020 7489 7920
Fax: 020 7489 1804
Email for national enquiries: national@fiac.org.uk
Email for London enquiries: london@fiac.org.uk
Website: www.fiac.org.uk

Guardian's Allowance Unit
Child Benefit Centre
DWP (Washington)
P O Box 1
Newcastle upon Tyne NE88 1AA

Tel: 0870 155 5540
Email: Child-Benefit@dwp.gsi.gov.uk
Website: www.dwp.gov.uk

Health Benefits Division
Sandyford House
Archbold Terrace
Jesmond
Newcastle Upon Tyne NE2 1DB

Tel: 0191 203 5555

The Highways Agency - Traffic, Safety and Environment Division
St Christophers House
Southwark Street
London SE1 OTE

Tel: 020 7921 4667
Fax: 020 7921 4411
Website: www.highways.gov.uk

Home Energy Efficiency Scheme (HEFS) - Wales
Tel: 0800 316 2815

Independent Living Fund
PO Box 183
Nottingham NG8 3RD

Tel: 0115 942 8191 or 0115 942 8192

Inland Revenue Contributions Office
Inland Revenue
National Insurance Contributions Office
Benton Park View
Newcastle upon Tyne NE98 1ZZ

Tel: 0191 213 5000
Self Employment Services Call Centre: 0845 915 4655

Invalid Care Allowance (ICA) Unit
Palatine House
Lancaster Road
Preston PR1 1NS

Tel: 01253 856 123
Minicom: 01772 899 489
Website: www.dwp.gov.uk

Law Centre Northern Ireland
124 Donegal Street
Belfast BT1 2GY

Tel: 028 9024 4401
Fax: 028 9023 6340
Email: lawcentre.belfast@cinni.org

Law Centres Federation
Duchess House
18-19 Warren Street
London W1P 5DB

Tel: 020 7387 8570
Fax: 020 7387 8368
Email: info@lawcentres.org.uk
Website: www.lawcentres.org.uk

The Law Society
113 Chancery Lane
London WC2A 1PL

Tel: 020 7242 1222
Fax: 020 7831 0344
Email: info.services@lawsociety.org.uk
Website: www.lawsoc.org.uk

Legal Aid Board - Scotland
44 Drumsheugh Gardens
Edinburgh EH3 7SW

Tel: 0131 226 7061
Website: www.slab.org.uk

The Macfarlane Trust
PO Box 627
London SW1H 0HG

Tel: 020 7233 0342
Fax: 020 7233 0839
Website: www.medicine.ox.ac.uk/ohc/mactrust.htm

Minimum Income Guarantee Claim Line
Tel: 0800 028 1111

Motability
Goodman House
Station Approach
Harlow
Essex CM20 2ET

Tel: 01279 635 666

Motor Insurers' Bureau (MIB)
152 Silbury Boulevard
Central Milton Keynes MK9 1NB

Tel: 01908 830 001

National Assembly for Wales Highways Directorate
Cathays Park
Cardiff CF1 3NQ

Tel: 01222 826 482
Fax: 01222 823 792
Website: www.wales.gov.uk

National Association of Citizens Advice Bureaux
Myddelton House
115- 123 Pentonville Road
London N1 9LZ

Tel: 020 7833 2181
Fax: 020 7833 4371
Website: www.nacab.org.uk

National Centre for Independent Living
250 Kennington Lane
London SE11 5RD

Tel: 020 7587 1663
Fax: 020 7582 2469
Minicom: 020 7587 1177
Email: ncil@ncil.demon.co.uk

National Union of Students
Nelson Mandela House
461 Holloway Road
London N7 6LJ

Tel: 020 7272 8900
Fax: 020 7263 5713
Email: nusuk@nus.org.uk
Website: www.nusonline.co.uk

Pensions Infoline
Tel: 0845 731 3233

Portset Systems Ltd
Brook Street
Bishops Waltham
Southamption SO32 1AX

Tel : 01489 893 919
Fax: 01489 893 320
General email address:
admin@portset.co.uk
Website: www.portset.co.uk/us.htm

The Prince's Trust
Head Office
18 Park Square East
London NW1 4LH

Tel: 020 7543 1234
Fax: 020 7543 1200
Textphone: 020 7543 1374
Website: www.princes-trust.org.uk

Redundancy Payments Office
Helpline: 0500 848 489

Office for Scotland, Cleveland, Cumbria, Durham, Merseyside, Northumberland, Teesside, Tyne and Wear, Yorkshire

Department of Trade and Industry
Redundancy Payments Office
Ladywell House
Ladywell Road
Edinburgh EH12 7UR

Tel: 0131 316 5600

Office for Buckinghamshire, Essex, Hertfordshire, Kent, London, Suffolk, Surrey, Sussex

PO Box 15
Exchange House
60 Exchange Road
Watford WD1 7SP

Tel: 01923 210 700

Office for Wales and all other counties in England

7th Floor Hagley House
83-85 Hagley Road
Birmingham B16 8QG

Tel: 0121 456 4411

Retirement Pensions Tele- Claim Service
The Pensions Service

Tel: 0845 300 1084
Website: www.thepensionservice.gov.uk

Scottish Association of Law Centres
Paisley Law Centre
65 George Street
Paisley PA1 2JY

Tel: 0141 561 7164

Scottish Executive
St. Andrew's House
Regent Road
Edinburgh EH1 3DG

Enquiry Line: 0845 774 1741
Minicom: 0131 244 1829
Email (Enquiries): ceu@scotland.gov.uk Fax: 0131 244 8240
Website: www.scotland.gov.uk

Scottish Executive Development Department
Victoria Quay
Edinburgh EH6 6QQ

Tel: 0131 244 7225
Fax: 0131 244 7228
Website: www.scotland.gov.uk

Scottish Legal Aid Board
44 Drumsheugh Gardens
Edinburgh EH3 7SW

Website: www.slab.org.uk

The Scottish Office Development Department
Victoria Quay
Edinburgh EH6 6QQ

Tel: 0131 556 8400

The Student Awards Agency for Scotland (SAAS)
Gyleview House
3 Redheughs Rigg
Edinburgh EH12 9HH

Tel: 0131 476 8212
Website: www.student-support-saas.gov.uk

Tax Credit Office
Inland Revenue
PO Box 145
Dorchester House
Preston PR1 0GP

Working Families' Tax Credit helpline: 0845 609 5000
Disabled Person's Tax Credit helpline: 0845 605 5858
Inland Revenue website: www.inlandrevenue.gov.uk

Telephone Helplines Association
4 Deans Court
St Paul's Churchyard
London EC4V 5AA

Tel: 020 7248 3388
Fax: 020 7248 3399
Email: Info@helplines.org.uk
Website: www.helplines.org.uk

Vaccine Damage Payments Unit
Palatine House
Lancaster Road
Preston PR1 1HB

Tel: 01722 237 800

Veterans Agency
Norcross
Blackpool FY5 3WP

Veterans Helpline: 0800 169 2277
Website: www.veteransagency.mod.uk

The Warm Deal
Eaga Limited
Freepost SCO 4421
Edinburgh EH6 0BR

Tel: 0800 072 0150
Minicom: 0800 072 0156
Website: www.scotland.gov.uk/housing/leaflets/wdfs-00.asp

The Warm Front Team
Health Energy Efficiency Scheme for England
National Office
St. Andrew's House
90-92 Pilgrim Street
Newcastle Upon Tyne NE1 6SG

Tel: 0800 072 0600
Email: fuel.poverty@defra.gsi.gov.uk.

Winter Fuel Payment Helpline
Tel: 0845 915 1515
Textphone: 0845 974 5136

Index